TOUCHSTONE

$2.66 5 N 577 3

working mothers

working mothers

by JEAN CURTIS

A TOUCHSTONE BOOK
PUBLISHED BY SIMON AND SCHUSTER

ACKNOWLEDGMENTS

I wish to thank, first, the more than two hundred busy women who agreed to talk with me about their lives, and the issues they faced as working mothers. I thank them because, of course, they provided the substance, the truths, of this book; also because they were warm, often fun, and willing to discuss personal, sometimes highly sensitive matters with a stranger who could promise them nothing but honest attention.

I also thank their families—their husbands and children—many of whom were willing to tell me *their* side, what it is like to live with a working mother.

Kate Medina, my editor, and Lois Wallace, my agent, provided the inspiration for this book, and I am pleased and grateful that they did.

Grateful acknowledgment is also made to the following for their kind permission to reprint material from copyright sources:

William Morrow & Company, Inc., extracts from *Man's World, Woman's Place,* © by Elizabeth Janeway, 1971; The Dial Press, extract from *The Future of Motherhood,* © by Jessie Bernard, 1974; The Washington *Post,* extract from "The State of the Fatherland and the Comfort of Continuity," by Colman McCarthy, June 17, 1973; The New American Library, extract from *Voices from Women's Liberation,* © by Leslie B. Tanner, 1970; The New York *Times,* extract from two editions, January 6, 1975 and January 20, 1975; *Pediatrics,* extract from "Effects of Maternal Employment on the Child," by Mary C. Howell, September, 1973.

Finally I wish to thank my husband, Michael, for reasons best known to him.

Manufactured in the United States of America

1 2 3 4 5 6 7 8 9 10

Library of Congress Cataloging in Publication Data

Curtis, Jean, date.
Working mothers.

(A Touchstone book)
1. Mothers—Employment—United States.   2. Children
of working mothers.   I. Title.
[HD6055.C87   1977]   301.42'7   76-53776
ISBN 0-671-22753-X

For Alma Reinertsen
and Ruth Reinertsen Getchell,
my grandmother,
my mother. With love.

PREFACE

When I set out to write this book about working mothers, I wasn't sure whether working mothers were cruel destroyers of childhood—or a legion of society's noblest and least appreciated heroines—or somewhere in between these extremes. My own experience as a working mother was limited, and I was not at all sure I even knew which of the questions people raised, pro and con, were the important ones. But I knew that whenever the subject came up—mother: to work or not to work—that subject then came to dominate the conversation; and that conversation would rapidly become heated. Having some special interest in the subject myself, I was more than willing to be educated through writing this book. And educated I was.

My own work as a writer had, for several years, been done at home; my writing schedule had been gingerly wrapped around the demands of my family and my house. I was—and am—the mother of three children, two who were in school and a third who was still (both figuratively and literally) in my lap, when work on this book began. My oldest child was seven in 1970, when I ended a painfully stagnant period of my life to write my first book.

I timed that project so that the actual writing began shortly after my third child was born, and I alternated, I thought rather gracefully, between the typewriter and an infant I felt sure sensed that his mother was doing something she felt was particularly productive. At eighteen months, Hans attended a playgroup two mornings a week, and by the time he was two and a half, he was going to a nursery school five days a week—and loving it. He was

three when I started research for this book and will be five before
it is published.

I've had my own misgivings about motherhood during the past
two years as a working mother, and I've been fascinated by the
lives of women who were working longer hours than I was, and
who seemed to be holding their own both on the job and at
home. What I thought I would learn from interviewing working
mothers gradually became something altogether different. I had
been looking for stress and anxiety; and I found, certainly, some
of both. But the sources of the tension were not always what I
had thought they would be.

I interviewed over two hundred women, their husbands, and
children. They came from various sections of the United States,
and from various backgrounds. Most interviews lasted for at least
an hour; some for several hours. The names have been changed in
this book out of respect for privacy, and in modest ways personal
details have been altered so as not to be needlessly revealing. I
have promised anonymity to everyone who sought it—a promise
which enabled the talk to flow more freely.

Within a month or two of the beginning of my research, I had
more prospective interviewees than I could manage: women
wanted to talk. And many of their husbands were curious, too,
and anxious to contribute. The children were full of enthusiasm.

I owe a great deal to the women who talked with me. I was increasingly amazed at how forthright women were willing to be—
with a total stranger, a woman they might never see again. Sometimes it was clear that the fact that I was a "stranger" enabled the
talk to be more frank. One woman in Connecticut told me, "I
wish I could see you again. I think we have a lot to say to each
other." I wish the same for all these women and hope this book
will prove a reward of sorts for their time and frankness. But I
think the main reason so many women, and men, were willing to
talk to me was their sharp concern over the quandry raised by the
questions: Should a mother work or not? If she does, what does it
do to the children? The husband? The marriage? What does it do
for—or to—the woman herself? How do the mothers—and their
families—cope? For many women, and men, these questions are
among the most important questions of the day.

What might be considered "true" answers five or ten years ago
don't seem so true today. One thing the interviews for this book

confirmed is that times have changed! Interests and concerns about the family have changed. This book speaks to these interests and concerns. Aside from an occasional "how to do it" book, I've found no body of literature that addresses itself to the problems of working mothers and their families. I have tried, in this book, to bring together a number of insights, the commonsense working out of the situation. It is my hope that these perspectives, never before co-ordinated, will benefit families who now, or in the future, face the dovetailing issues of vocation and parenthood. For the stress and anxiety of any social change is often painfully isolated behind the doors of warmly lit homes—and the fact is, today, one of the greatest social changes going on concerns women, their families, and work.

CONTENTS

working mothers

one

GETTING SOME NEW ADVICE:
THE OLD TRADITIONS DIE HARD

For even when there is large agreement that women have a perfect right to work if they want to, as there is today, the effort to change customs and institutions may lag very considerably because of the mythic residue at the bottom of our minds. We don't try hard enough. 'All right, let them work if they want to,' has a bit of an echo of 'Let them eat cake' to it. It encourages, by complacency, that effective method of heading off any push for change by assuring the world that the change has already taken place, that women have all the rights they need, or at least as much as is good for them and for their families. (. . . Closed minds accept myth most easily, but a frightened society seeks it actively.) ELIZABETH JANEWAY, Man's World, Woman's Place, *Morrow, 1971*

Ten years ago, referring in her first paragraph of *The Feminine Mystique* to the life of a housewife, Betty Friedan asked, "Is this all?" In the past ten years more women have read that question and wondered about it than Friedan could ever have expected.

Some women found the answer annoying—especially at first. They placed a high value on the time they spent with children and home. The life of a homemaker, housewife, mother, they felt, is a rich life, and one that women can uniquely benefit from. Moreover, it is one in which women have unique power to mold and raise future generations, to affect strongly the people they most love. In response to Friedan's question, many parried, "Isn't this enough?"

Other women read Friedan's book with less conviction that their lives had taken the shape they were most comfortable with. They carried Friedan's question to bed with them at night and wondered, when the lights were out and everyone was bathed, pajamaed, brushed, fed, and warmly asleep, why they felt so uneasy. "Is this all?" they echoed. "Can it be?"

In the past decade more and more women with both views have moved out of their homes to find work. They have needed to work—either to help support their families or to support their own sense of themselves in a world they have been educated to take a practical and philosophical interest in.

Whatever social, economic, political, or psychological reasons seem to explain this phenomenon, statistics demonstrate that working mothers are on the rise—according to the U. S. Department of Labor statistics, there are 14 million working mothers in the United States today. As a consequence, family roles may be changing once again.

In 1960 barely 19 per cent of mothers with children under the age of five worked outside their homes for a salary. By 1972 the figure was 45 per cent, according to the U. S. Department of Labor statistics. In 1960, 39 per cent of mothers with children of school age were gainfully employed. Twelve years later the figure was up to 57 per cent. In 1975 an estimated 51 per cent of mothers with preschool children were working full time, outside their homes, in salaried positions. And, experts tell us, the number increases every day.

This rapid rise in the number of mothers who work is causing a struggle in millions of homes. Couples need to find some new compromises in order to fit their modern and very busy lives into the strictures of family life.

It used to be that, when a couple got married, certain compromises were expected—indeed, were rarely questioned. The most fundamental, perhaps, was the assumption, by both, of sexual monogamy. By and large, this meant that the man would compromise his limitless, impersonal drives and the woman, in return, would provide him with a home and bed worthy of his sacrifice. In return for her nurturing, he would work hard and in time they could achieve a standard of living within range of their expectations. Children would eventually appear and the wife would take over the rearing of the offspring. For a long time, at least for a few hundred years, it was a relatively peaceful arrangement.

Although this concept of marriage and family life is changing very slowly, the number of working mothers is increasing all the time. For the most part, women who are working are working because their families can no longer expect to live as they would like to with only one salary. So the motivation for change in husband and wife roles comes, for many, from without—not from inner emotional or psychological reasons. For others, the seeds of discontent planted in their *minds* since Friedan have not flowered into any actual changes in the way they live their lives. Still others have been trying to work, for complex personal reasons.

Whatever the reasons for a mother's working, as a consequence many couples find their lives changing in a number of ways. Their day-to-day work loads have altered—she is preoccupied with trying to balance child care and work responsibilities, while he finds he is needed more for household matters and child care than he ever expected to be. They have to mold new views of themselves as regards work—she begins to see herself as a serious contributor to the family income; he begins to realize he doesn't have to carry the whole financial burden himself. Women enjoy increased career opportunities—affirmative action plans in factory and university have brought blue-collar and white-collar women new benefits and status. In some cases, though not most, both husband and wife find childrearing responsibilities shifting—she tries to move over to allow for child care and paternal influence; he finds he's expected to share more of the day-to-day concerns about baby or child.

Yet many of the couples I talked with had not changed the traditional basic assumptions about what a mother and father, a husband and wife, are supposed to be to each other and to their children. The daily facts of their lives had changed radically; their perceptions of their roles and routines had not caught up with that reality.

If a wife is gone from her home as often as her husband, conflicts are bound to occur if both assume that things ought to go on as before. Both husband and wife are tired at the end of the day and face children who, though tired too, need *both* parents.

Nevertheless, despite rhetoric and logic, in my interviews I found that the management of the house and the raising of the children is still seen by almost everyone as primarily the job of the mother; that she may also be working as hard as her husband at her other job is an added responsibility—and usually a secondary one—in *her* mind, too. Children, from time to time, present pressing needs of which working mothers are painfully aware, yet many of the women I talked to were handicapped by the examples set by their own mothers, and by their youthful fantasies of what it would be like to be married and raise children. Conflicts of this sort demand a new set of compromises between a husband and wife: the guidelines for these compromises are not written down in any book. Such couples have little to fall back on. Where are the new rules?

Because no body of literature has existed to help couples adjust to changing roles, women have been struggling to maintain two treadmills, often to the detriment of both. To my surprise, I found that this situation hasn't changed very much. Marriage and family life have seen havoc thrown on what most people thought was a good social system—the nuclear family. In the wake of this storm, psychologists, psychiatrists, pediatricians have written with skepticism about the problems working mothers impose on their children and husbands, and suggested that women ought to return to the kitchen in order to preserve the American family, to save children from neglect and neurosis, and husbands from uncertainty and despair.

The fact is that if the women I talked to indicate a general trend, women are not apt to return home, at least not until after 5 P.M. Telling them to, a heaping on of the guilt, has not solved the problem. So what do working mothers do? If couples can no longer meet the demands of a traditional marriage, how are they adjusting to new realities? Where do they go for help?

Although many books have been published about new life styles —how to break out of corporate life, how to live in communes, start a food co-op, raise your level of consciousness, have an open marriage, or an exciting sex life—the literature that couples turn to when they need advice about children and family life has not changed much at all. *Baby and Child Care*, by Dr. Benjamin Spock was first published in 1946. Slightly revised, it still stands as the bible of pediatric advice to parents. Working mothers and

nonworking mothers alike still turn to it to discover when their
first child should learn to walk and why he has spots on his stomach. They get comforting advice on both counts, such as the following:

> It's time to go in for lunch, but your small child is digging happily
> in the dirt. . . . He just gets balky right away, disagreeably balky. I'd
> pick him up casually and carry him indoors, even if he's squealing and
> kicking like a little pig. You do this in a self-confident way. . . . A
> small child who is feeling miserable and making a scene is comforted
> underneath by sensing that his mother knows what to do without
> getting angry.

Many couples today would have been happier if Spock had
included fathers in this scene; nevertheless, his words of reassur-
ance are just what most parents are looking for. Other pediatric
literature rarely comes on with a good second act—not after a
parent has already read it all in Spock.

Spock, dear Spock, gave us the ammunition to feel self-
confident when confronted with our own children. He has not,
however, given us the same self confidence in our private lives—
when we are not supervising the sandbox directly, but contemplating raising children without ever having much to do with a sandbox ourselves. What do a woman and a man do when they live in
a high-rise apartment house, work full time, send their baby to a
day-care center, and try to discover each other over a weekend?
For this hypothetical couple, Spock is simply outdated.*

Spock is not alone—pediatric literature still is written with an
underlying assumption that it is the mother who is overseeing
every moment of a child's development. This assumption affects
just about every source of pediatric advice available. If a young
parent needs to know what to do when an eleven-month-old re-
fuses to eat anything but peanut butter and raisins and cries all
day, the advice in the books does not suggest that a parent speak
to the day-care teacher, the housekeeper, the live-in baby-sitter, or
the playgroup leader. The advice will tell the *mother* how to handle that baby in a way which lets the mother know *she* alone can
handle such a situation; the "Spockian" authors know that
women as mothers need self-confidence more than they need prac-

---

* In 1976, after *Working Mothers* was published, Dr. Spock revised his *Baby
and Child Care* to "eliminate sexist biases" he felt were in earlier editions.
"Now I recognize that the father's responsibility is as great as the mother's,"
he says, and he takes pains to assure women that they have a right to work.

tical knowledge, because that's what they have the least of—self-confidence.

The reason Spock and other less well-known doctors have been so influential, presumably, is that most people haven't been trained very well for their roles as parents. Women in particular have tended to assume that their individual needs must be repressed in favor of the needs of their children. A common assumption, but what of all the women who must now work? They have to see that the needs of their children are met by someone else for some part of the day, or, at the very least, that their children hold onto their problems until 6 P.M. when both parents get in the door. Childrearing problems, questions, the very real concern for children's welfare are different for the working mother than the problems faced by women who are in their homes all day.

Who *are* these people who research childrearing problems? For the most part they have been male pediatricians. For the most part they have been kindly and very concerned for the welfare of children. They have been sympathetic to the problems women have had as housewives and mothers, yet they have been puzzled by the occasional woman who insists she can be mother and architect at the same time. Much of the research for these books stems from a belief in a traditional nuclear family. A maternal influence and presence in the home is assumed. Where do parents with different assumptions or family arrangements go for help?

Child psychologists have been warning mothers that their children are going to pay a price if the mother works out of the home for eight hours a day. Dr. Lee Salk, director of pediatric psychology at the New York Hospital-Cornell Medical Center, told *People* magazine that it was difficult for a woman to have a successful career and be a successful mother at the same time. "But it's possible for both parents to work if they have a schedule that, at least for the first three years, enables one parent to spend a few hours with the child in the middle of the day."

For many working parents this advice isn't practical. "All I can say is that I'm an advocate for children, not mothers and fathers," Salk says. In the same article he states that if women want to work and have a child too, well, "that's like saying they'd like to be a full-time skier and a full-time professor. They can't do both effectively. I can't tell you how many disturbed children result from that situation."

My research for this book suggests that the accepted premise of many doctors is wrong. Disturbed children are to be found in families where the mother works—beyond question. But where is the evidence that they do not occur just as frequently in homes where only one parent, usually the father, is working? If the women I've talked with are a valid cross-section, Dr. Salk and others are guilty of gravely oversimplifying the problem that is the working mother's greatest source of guilt. Among the families I interviewed, only a handful had children who were not adjusting to school as well as other children. Statistically speaking, their experience could indicate that Salk's thesis is not valid.

Dr. Spock's book *Raising Children in a Difficult Time* (Norton, 1974) is full of understanding comments about human fallibility and complexity. Nevertheless, he, like many of his colleagues, can lead working parents into some blind alleys.

Spock's chapter about the "father's role" acknowledges that many fathers "don't play with their children because they don't feel comfortable doing it." That, in Spock's view, is all right. Better, he thinks, that a child strives to be an adult with adult interests than that an adult strive to succeed in the world of a child. Many women would agree!

And many working mothers have noticed that their children begin to try harder to be an adult, and can live equally with this impetus when it comes from two role models in the family. Having two working parents, some have discovered, reinforces that drive, which may leave less room for conflict over future ambitions and professional paths.

Dr. Spock writes in his 1974 book that a father, "during the hours when he is at home," should take part in the care of his child. But, he adds, "we have to face the fact, however, that there are still millions of fathers today who have not participated much in the care of their children. . . . The first question is whether the children will suffer as a consequence of this lack of relationship. *Not necessarily.* A child can admire and gain inspiration from a father who is so dignified or so unhandy at making things or so uninterested in sports and nature that he can't enjoyably do any of these things, if father and child are reasonably comfortable with each other and can talk spontaneously at the dinner table from time to time."

Dr. Spock frequently salvages the hypothetical father or husband from shame and distress by painting him as so dignified, so picturesque, such a nice fellow that women readers may have responded as much to that image of their husbands as they responded to their own needs—needs they were continually being told they ought to repress for the sake of their children. But working mothers who are facing daily the real world of work, the real expectations of a boss, the real fact of bills to be paid, the real fact of husband and doctor who wish mothers would stay home, or at least *pretend* to stay home—these women, working mothers who now number 14 million, are in need of more support from experts, more help from their husbands, and more understanding from a world that agrees only to tolerate them. At what point does a mother's need for reliable, committed participation in the parenting process take precedence over the quaintness of fatherly helplessness? There's never been anything quaint about a *mother* who can't change diapers, cook three meals a day, keep a clean and orderly house, administer to the emotional needs of her family and find time, in odd moments, to explore her own private initiatives, professional or otherwise. Many of the fathers I talked to had begun to share more equally the responsibilities of parenthood, and had wished they'd done so from the beginning.

The problem, my interviews seem to suggest, is not how much work is done, or how much time away from their children parents have to surrender to work. Rather, the problem seems to lie as much in the way parents deal with the life shaped by that work schedule. A new set of compromises has to be learned, and not only by parents. The children have to compromise too. And employers may eventually learn why such compromises are valuable.

Some women, I found, who had already raised their children while holding down a full-time job had never questioned a traditional family arrangement that had, they felt, made sense for them. These women, over forty and still working, now had the benefit of hindsight and a view of their lives within the framework of the women's movement and the changing times. For the most part, these women had stayed home for a number of years (eight to ten) in order to raise two or three children until the youngest was in first grade. Then they had picked up their careers and carried on with the aid of a housekeeper, a firm sense of self-confidence in their mothering, and a very good standard of living.

Ingrid, one of these women, was forty-six when I met her. Her children were fourteen, seventeen, and nineteen. She was earning $23,000 as a clinical psychologist, working four days a week. She readily admits that if she were a young woman now, she wouldn't be able to do it the same way. She had stayed home for eight years before returning to graduate school to finish her Ph.D. and begin her professional life.

Ingrid felt, as did many other women her age, that women who stayed home for such a period were "getting the best of both worlds." She didn't have the feeling of having compromised her family, although, she said uneasily, "I have the feeling of having compromised my job. . . ."

Ingrid felt she had never taken her professional identity as seriously as she might. "So that even when I *was* a working mother, by the outside standards I had some degree of status; it really wasn't something that I accepted or communicated to the family." In fact, Ingrid viewed herself as "tied up" with her husband, a professor of chemistry. *He,* she told me, traveled in a world of "very high intellectual accomplishment." Anything she did in comparison seemed pale. "When I brought myself back to the household, or even to our social world, mainly chemists, I was never very impressed with myself. So I would play down my work."

Ingrid was aware that her professional ambitions were modified by the fact that she was a mother. She was on two treadmills, she felt, the treadmill of work and the treadmill of home. She had very little time for anything else.

"I remember saying glibly when I first went back to work that I prided myself on never running out of toilet paper. What I do now is to get full-time help. My husband did nothing. He never took an interest. If you'd ask him, I think he would say he helped out, and maybe he did, but 'psychologically' the household has always been my job. My husband is a nice guy and he doesn't harbor any attitudinal stuff. I suspect I, as much as anyone, held to the assumption that the running of the house and the caring of the children were my responsibilities."

Ingrid admits that what she settled for—a happy home, a late-blooming career, a nice guy, enough money to travel at will—is not what the new generation is after.

"I down-played my ambition and accomplishments. With my talents I could have done much more. I did my work well. I was always reliable and responsible, but in most professions that is not enough to get ahead. There has to be that extra push, that extra bit of ambition and freedom that makes one more creative. The women of my generation, as a rule, did not accomplish that much —even gifted people just accepted, and not necessarily unhappily (I want to underline that). The younger generation, it seems to me, won't stand for that."

The conventional pediatric wisdom on this subject is that if you are so ambitious that you are unwilling to put aside a few years of your career to have children, then you shouldn't have children. Many Americans, for that matter, are realizing they don't need or want children for just that reason. But for every two "non-parents," hundreds of others are unprepared, unwilling, or unable to forsake parenthood. And so they have babies.

Many ambitious, aggressive, talented women in America are getting married to ambitious, aggressive, talented men. A lot of these couples want to have children; and they don't want to compromise their careers in the process. A way has to be found for these people to cope, because if there isn't, our society's whole family structure may rapidly fall apart. Where the element of choice is not involved and both parents or a single parent must work for reasons of economic survival, the argument for accommodation is even more urgent.

Ingrid talked about the women's movement in a way that emphasizes how much society is changing, whether or not we approve of the transformation.

"Women's liberation has absolutely fit into my life. I haven't joined any groups or anything like that, but it's out there. You can't miss it. I think it changes your perception of the world and of yourself. These changes are supported by whatever one reads and by the attitudes that are just in the air. One of the most important things women's liberation does is support one's sense of self worth. I'm not one who complains. I mean I don't look at any of this and scream with rage at what might have been, because I'm really not unhappy with the way I've handled things. I'm not bitter, and I get a little annoyed at some of the bitterness that I hear, because I think it's naïve to be bitter about it. These things are part of a larger historical process. *It's part of the changing times.* The changes that are taking place are the movements of history and society."

Women younger than Ingrid who have been through the rigors of consciousness-raising groups speak of their feelings about time spent away from a career and with children in terms of anger.

These women, in their thirties now, have much in common with Ingrid. They often dabbled in some sort of independent life prior to their marriage—a year in a job in New York City, a year in Europe. They thought of themselves as "savvy" women. Ingrid, however, had more distance in which to view her decisions and spoke of them wistfully:

"Two years after we were married, we moved to Chicago, and the most independent thing I ever did in my whole life was to leave my husband, who was working at the university there, and go to New York for six weeks to collect data for my thesis. It was then that I came to the dramatic conclusion that I was hardly a professional woman. I hated this business of being alone in New York. I went back and got pregnant, deliberately. I just didn't like that role . . . I wasn't very ambitious. That's an important ingredient in the way I was able to make it all work out. But there was an internal conflict that I wasn't aware of. . . . I think I was scared.

"I went straight from home to marriage. I had very little of independent life. Now that didn't happen to all women in my generation, but I think it's safe to say that on the whole, we didn't lead independent lives. We didn't strike out on our own. We went from the dependence of being at home to the dependence on our husbands. If there's anything I tell my daughters, it's that they should have that period of independence before they get married. Girls and boys are given the kind of independence now I never had."

All the women I interviewed who were over forty told me that the difference between their generation and the young women currently in their twenties—those who supposedly would reap the rewards of the women's movement—was that those over forty had no real conflict. They had never questioned their obligation to stay home and rear their children. That role was universally expected of them—even their professors expected them to go from the classroom to the maternity ward, into the kitchen and nursery. They were grateful for their education, and those with real ambitions swallowed them for a time, then tried to pick up where they left off.

One of Ingrid's colleagues, a physician who had taken twelve years after her residency to rear three children, also followed the traditional pattern.

"I got pregnant after my residency and my O.B. told me to stay off my feet. I was doing surgery at the time, and so had no choice. I stopped working. By the time I thought I was ready to resume my residency, number two was coming. So once again, I had to stay off my feet for a few months. Then I had two children. My husband and I talked it over and decided that the children would either be housekeeper's children or my children. Naturally I didn't want them to be housekeeper's children. So I stayed home. My husband left it up to me. He said you do whatever you think you should do. I didn't think it was fair to have children and then not give them the best you could, and besides that, I like children. I enjoyed them. It wasn't punishment at all."

The assumption that if you don't stay home with your children, they won't be your children, won't have your values, won't know what it's like to have close family relationships, a "one to one" maternal tie, is at the root of the dilemma. Most women still see children and working in either/or terms—and most husbands encourage this view. Some, however, cling doggedly to the belief that a woman can manage it all, be superwoman, supermom, and super career woman. They sacrifice free time, leisure, athletic or social activities, and ultimately a sense of inner peace or tranquility.

Is a mother right to work? Does a mother have a right to work? These are questions mothers and fathers and a great many other people are asking themselves in face of the *fact* of working mothers—the questioning still goes on—and in the face of great distress and anxiety in many homes.

The old traditions are being questioned, all right—but they die hard. Some of the main anxieties of the working-mother situation continue to be fears about the following:

Is it possible that it's true that children forced off the maternal lap "too soon" will not be as independent and secure as their peers who are coddled by mothers willing to give them years of constant care? I discovered that fostering independence in children could be directly related to how much rein children are given—and how soon.

Are working wives (mothers) tempted to withdraw from their

homes once they are exposed to the allures of the working world? Many people assume that extramarital sex is a real threat if the wife works. I wanted to find out if that was fact or fiction.

Do women work because they want to escape their children? I didn't know, but I did want to examine the question of why women want to work. Are all working mothers ambitious and aggressive?

How hard is it for women to face getting back into the work force? I wanted to find out *when* it was hardest and when, if ever, it was relatively easy. Why did some women glide effortlessly into a profession, and others always seem to be swimming upstream?

Is this myth about working mothers true—that a wife who leaves her kitchen and nursery in the hands of hired help is neither domestic, maternal, nor wifely?

Mothers who want to work won't find much comfort in the child-care books that purport to help them. The experts, up to now, haven't done much homework, or have taken too seriously the mythologies that have shaped our common heritage.

This book is based not on "expert's" advice, but on the commonsense solutions some working mothers have—painfully— worked out in answer to some of these questions.

two

MOTHERS WHO DO AND MOTHERS WHO DON'T: SOME ATTITUDES THAT AFFECT THEM BOTH

If the career mother is presaging the future, closely followed by the working mother with a job, the remaining half of mothers of school-age children, who are not in the labor force, are—some of them in any event—fighting a rear-guard action to preserve the status quo with a few of them even waging an aggressive campaign against the future.
JESSIE BERNARD, *The Future of Motherhood*, Dial Press, 1974

Mothers who work are controversial people. They evoke strong feelings, often much to their own surprise. People ask, "What do you think about *it?*" "Do you think it's a good thing?" By implication they suggest that it's a controversial topic, a situation about which one *needs* to have an opinion. You're either for or against working mothers in much the same way you're either for or against the use of nuclear energy. And whichever side a woman is on, pro or con, she will often find herself on the defensive, if not overtly—that is, when called upon to explain herself—then implicitly, as she feels the pressure of public skepticism.

For years some women have worked because they had to, either to support a family or to assure a standard of living commensurate with family expectations. Working mothers, and their problems, existed long before the women's movement brought them into sharper focus and shed new light on a situation many people viewed as unfortunate and/or unnatural. Now, day care and other child-related issues have become national issues. But feminist rhetoric has also heightened the pressure on working mothers—pressure which helps to make going back to work so hard. Public apprehension—the fear that wide use of day-care centers and the gradual erosion of housewifery will endanger marriage, the nuclear family, and the emotional as well as physical health of children—it's a big cause of censureship working mothers feel.

In only certain situations has a mother in this society been able to work without censure. If a family is poor or the mother is the only supporter—okay. And society takes more kindly, on the whole, to mothers in the high status professions (medicine, academia), particularly if they subordinate ambition to family responsibilities. But if a woman asserts, simply, that she has the same professional ambitions as her husband, that she shares his lack of interest in committing long hours to the management of the home or the care of the children, but would like, instead, to *share* those responsibilities (not duck them), she will swiftly learn the price of her adventurousness.

The identity wrapped up in the word *mother* may be more potent, more connotative, than meanings commonly attached to female or male, married or single, employed or unemployed, child or adult, husband or wife, rich or poor, and certainly father. In the psychological testing game that asks people to name the first word that comes to mind in response to certain other words, one can imagine something like the following associations: pencil—paper; car—road; book—read; food—eat; father—work; mother—home. Mother—lap. Mother—love. Mother—food. Mother—warm.

Mothers who violate the popular belief that they should stay in the home have been subject to subtle, and sometimes not so subtle, indictments.

Ironically, the women's movement has tended to heighten that prejudice. Working mothers now are often suspected of radicalism as well as mere neglect. One woman who had been working for twenty years told me that until recently no one ever mentioned it to her. "I was still a woman and mother first in everyone's eyes and got lumped, socially, with the rest of my sex. But now people often ask me why or how I did it. It's rather disconcerting—as if I were a different person than the one they'd been seeing for years."

Many women agree with her. They feel more scrutinized currently, and they're not comfortable with the feeling. The issue, however, has always been there. Women over forty with grown children have told me how they "hardened" themselves years ago to social disapproval. One woman from Cleveland, a social worker, told me:

"As a working mother I would often get a reaction from other women like, 'Oh, you work, and what do you do with your children?' The obvious implication was, 'Oh, those poor children.' I remember one time saying, flatly, 'I neglect them.'

"The other reaction I would get, when we had a dinner party, was that my guests were surprised I could put on a good table, that I could cook well, that the house was pretty and I was charming. They would say, 'I never thought of you as domestic!' The implication seemed clear: If you're a career woman, you're obviously a lousy mother and a lousy homemaker. I used to feel defensive about that. I probably went out of my way to prove I wasn't shirking my wifely duties."

A Cambridge woman remarked that when her child was five, and going to an expensive private school, all parent activities were held during school hours—so that mothers could attend. Divorced and working full time, she could rarely attend these events. One day a group of mothers approached her and asked her if she would be willing to give a talk to the kindergarten mothers at a coffee. "We wondered," they asked her, "if you would talk about what it's like as a working mother never to see your own child."

"I was so stunned," this working mother told me, "that I couldn't say anything. This came at a time, mind you, when I spent most of my day running from one place to another in order to be with Alexandra. I was with her every weekend, every waking moment, every evening, and had arranged my work hours so that I could have three afternoons a week with her. I thought I was with my daughter more than other mothers. But that group showed me how deeply felt the schism was between us. Now, five years later, many more of the mothers at the school work, and they often tell me how *they* feel 'different' towards the mothers who don't."

Women returning to work are apt to notice these attitudes right away. The first thing that may strike them is the loss of contact with old friends, mothers who stay at home. For many, of course, this is because of a busier schedule. They may not have time to spend an afternoon with a friend. Many of the changes in their lives are logistical. But as time wears on, many of these women find they have fewer and fewer opportunities to be with nonworking mothers.

"I really don't have any time for my friends. I never call them on the telephone. And they resent it. They stop calling me. Any relationship I had, with the exception of one or two with friends of recent vintage, is gone. And I'm sorry. In most cases the people I remain friendly with don't resent my working. Some people I'd been friendly with are terribly resentful of my working and don't understand the way I live. Some of my husband's friends—the men—are uncomfortable around me too. They won't treat me as an equal, worthy of normal conversational exchange."

This woman, with a Ph.D. in physics, was a dean at a women's college. Her husband, an electrical engineer, owned his own firm. She admitted feeling a sense of isolation attributable to her working. Part of that phenomenon, she felt, was due to changes in her own outlook. Nevertheless, the feelings were there and she was quick to point out that not all of her social problems came from other mothers.

"Being a working mother affects all sorts of social relationships. My biggest problem here on campus is with unmarried women. Most of the older tenured women are unmarried. When I first became interested in day-care centers and talked about them, my older colleagues said, 'Why should any of our money be spent on that? That's your problem, your children, you worry about them.' Those women are the worst chauvinists of all. They're the ones who don't mind having meetings all the time because they don't have anything else to do. That's one group I just don't deal with. It's the same thing with women who don't work. When I finally do get to call them, if I have a few minutes to spare, I feel funny. I feel like I have to make excuses for my failure to call earlier."

As we discussed why she felt guilty about friends who didn't work, she said she supposed she was on the defensive "because I feel disapproved of." Was that because they felt she was doing a poor job of mothering?

"No! No one has ever accused me of that and I don't feel that. A young woman comes to the house every day to care for the children and they are in fine shape. We live in a neighborhood with lots of other kids and my children have a very rich social life. I don't think it's disapproval of my mothering that I feel. It's something like this: I've stepped out of line. I haven't chosen their way. I obviously don't thrive on the things they are involved in. And I guess there's a sexual thing too—I seem to them to have the privileges of a man's world. I'm paid well and I don't eat peanut butter sandwiches for lunch, standing up in the kitchen."

Another woman who had been working for only a year and a half tried to define the subtle change she'd detected. She'd stayed home for eight years before going to graduate school for a teaching certificate. Amy lived in an old country house she and her husband had "worked on" for most of their married life. They had built a greenhouse off their kitchen and become expert horti-culturalists. In the summer they kept an organic garden and Amy was active in various environmental causes in town. Her return to graduate school was part time and barely disturbed the pattern of her life. Her first job in the local school system, however, proved another matter entirely.

"To be truthful, the only things I *noticed* during the first six months were that I was tired all the time and lost track of my hobbies. My house got dirtier, which is pretty sad, because I was never very good at house cleaning. The first time I noticed an uncomfortable feeling vis-à-vis my friends was during Christmas vacation. I wasn't included in some of the things I had taken part in before, little things like planning the neighborhood carolling for the children. I told myself that was because I had not been available so much. But then I began to seek out the women with whom I used to have at least a casual acquaintance, and I was surprised to find that after just a few months on the job, our relationship had changed. I found I couldn't just step in and take up where we had left off. They weren't as relaxed with me.

"By summer, the changes were more pronounced. Nobody called me at all and when I sought them out, I discovered I had been excluded. All their plans had been made and I realized with a thud that I had left the fold. Our group had an unspoken criterion for membership—that we all shared the same situation. We were housewives.

"Maybe that's just the way things are in life. You make a choice about how you are going to live, and then you find others who have made the same or similar choices and you feel comfortable with each other. Nevertheless, this discovery hurt my feelings, and I still feel lonely and excluded during vacations."

Another woman, a tenured professor at a midwestern women's

college, was philosophical about her situation. She felt she had always been considered as somewhat of an oddity in her neighborhood, a mindset which had protected her from a range of feminine community requests—making a cake for a bake sale, participating in a school book sale, the kind of intimate organizational affairs that women who didn't work participated in. At the same time there were moments when she sensed that these other mothers deliberately excluded her from participating even at the consumer end of the project because of their resentment of her.

"These mothers had little ways, I felt, of getting even with me. For example, they met to talk about how our playgroup was going, about problems of grabbing and sharing, about different children and how they were acting with each other. I, of course, would have been very interested to hear how my son was doing with the other children. But they didn't invite me.

"The college sponsored a book fair and one of these mothers was in charge of organizing it. I wasn't on the list to go . . . because it was for faculty wives. After the fair the kids were all bragging about it . . . what wonderful books and things and my older boy got very upset because he'd missed it. I was angry.

"Maybe I'm being unreasonable—wanting the best of both worlds. I don't really want to help them with their book fair, or do the playgroup, but I want to be *in on it*."

A Massachusetts woman with a live-in housekeeper to care for her children during the day, and do all her cleaning, told me how often other mothers took the time to suggest she might be having troubles with her children, even though her children were fine—happy well-adjusted little boys.

"Our housekeeper was going through one of her triannual crises and was feeling very down. I was aware of it, and my husband and I were talking about it, thinking about how it was affecting the children and so on. A neighbor saw me in the supermarket and remarked to me in a very bitchy way that my four-year-old son seemed 'depressed' and wasn't that to do with the fact that the housekeeper hadn't really seemed in as good spirits as she had in the beginning of the year. I started to worry. My son depressed? He happens to be one of the most cheerful human beings I've ever encountered and I didn't think he was, in fact, depressed. Maybe he had a cold or wasn't feeling just right, but 'depressed'?

No. This is one reason why my new friends are people who share roughly the same situation."

Women who work in professions previously dominated by males often feel they have to restrict their social life to people outside their place of employment. The wives of their colleagues find it difficult to accept them as friends, so they end up avoiding social contact outside of work.

Doris, a vice president at a large savings bank, was the only female executive in the company. She took pride in her singular achievement, but she was lonely and isolated on the job, and came home to still more isolation in her neighborhood.

"The wives of my colleagues seem to resent the amount of time I spend with their husbands. Even some of the men here are resentful of my presence—as if I were taking the job away from some deserving male. All the men at my level or above have men's clubs where they go for their lunch hour. The few men interested in me are usually single and very self-confident. They don't care if I'm a working mother but they don't seem to mind my talking about my children when we do have lunch or see each other outside of the office.

"My social life has to come from the people my husband meets at work or the occasional friendships I make with men and their wives who are much older than I am and very successful. These women, beyond the age of child-care responsibilities, are more likely to feel comfortable with me."

It isn't difficult to understand why a woman with a very successful career would be threatening to women who stay home with children. But that, in a sense, is a separate issue from what most working mothers mean when they talk about public censure. Most women told me they felt they were battling a set of convictions over maternal care. The best mothering, they pointed out, was considered full-time mothering. Anything less is that, less.

The argument is hard to resist without substantial proof. How can working mothers prove that they can be good mothers? As long as feelings over this issue lingered with them, women told me that they often felt they had to be *better* at mothering, and *better* at their jobs than other women. One woman who worked at a high-pressured job in New York City told me how she always made the effort to attend school functions for her daughters, even if they were scheduled at 3:00 in the afternoon and she had to postpone executive meetings at her office. Often these functions were teas for other mothers and their children to meet teachers and engage in social niceties. "So many times when I get there, I find that the events are poorly attended. I know that most of the other mothers don't work. So, I ask myself, where are they? The irony is that they don't feel they have to attend, so they don't. Little happenings like that continually remind me of what an edge I'm on, how hard I try to be all things in both of my lives."

Male attitudes toward working mothers are less troublesome to many women. The attitudes are, women say, expected—an extension of sexist struggle. Professional friction and on-the-job struggles for equality are things most working mothers deal with without the sting they feel when criticized by their own sex. Women can prove they are just as good as men at their jobs more easily than they can prove they are good mothers as well. When confronted with a woman who *believes* it is wrong to work while mothering, women who work feel isolated. How can a woman discuss her four-year-old's separation problems in nursery school without feeling the cold stare of "I told you so"?

Most women I talked to found that unless hostile male attitudes came from their own husbands, a situation they were obliged to confront, they simply let them wash over. "It's a social thing really," one woman said. "You can sense if a man has chauvinist attitudes and unless you feel belligerent at the moment, you tend to let it go by. I can imagine it's different if you're married to one. Then you've got to fight for your life . . . and I would."

Interestingly, male disapproval of working mothers, many women feel, is the result of chauvinism whereas disapproving female attitudes seem to be taken as a disagreement over parental obligations and style. Confronted with female disapproval, working mothers often told me they felt defensive and angry. When I asked them about male disapproval, they often broke into a sarcastic smile, deprecating the source of disapproval as relatively unimportant and perfectly predictable. Women's attitudes, it seemed to me, toward male disapproval are comparable to their attitudes toward unprofessional criticism.

Many working mothers appeared to be sensitive to media discussions of such issues as day-care or other child-care solutions, particularly when these discussions appear on the women's page and seem intended for consideration *by women only.* The emphasis, inevitably, will have to do with ways *women,* not husbands or families, can cope with the problems of working mothers.

A Filipino woman living in upstate New York with four young children told me that when she came to this country she looked forward to what she'd thought would be more relaxed American customs. She was a trained librarian and had positioned herself in a university community where she and her husband, a linguist, could work and her children could have a good education. Lea found that the problems were nearly the same here as in the Philippines. She read whatever she could about the women's movement and her rights as a working woman. She had this to say:

"Whenever I read a magazine piece or newspaper article about child care which calls for more and better day-care centers or government-funded centers 'so that *women* can return to work,' I bristle. Why don't they ever say we ought to have better and more day-care centers so that 'parents' can work more freely or something like that? The New York *Times* is always publishing articles, mostly written by women, that put the responsibility for child-care needs on women. The underlying assumption in these articles is that we women are responsible for the children, as if we conceived them without any help, as if we alone can take care of them. I'd like to see some interviews with men who wanted better and cheaper day care for their children so that they wouldn't have to worry about getting to work on time. *Then* I'd think liberation had really done its job."

Attitudes toward working mothers also affect a great many women who are *not* working. Many women who have chosen not to work, at least while their children are young, feel "the libber's eye" on them. "I can't stand to go to a party and have somebody ask me what I do," said one woman who had worked for seven years as a teacher before quitting to have a baby. She now has two children and hasn't worked for five years. She isn't at all sure she wants to go back to teaching, and is pretty sure she won't work, in any case, until both children are much older. "If I tell them I'm a housewife or a mother, I feel oddly defensive. Like I want to tell them that I'm not just goofing off. That I'm just as bright and interesting as they are."

Women with very ambitious husbands who expend most of their energies at work seem to face the same problem. Their social life, they told me, often consists chiefly of people who are always busy "working"—the kind of work, moreover, that is highly valued in our society. Women largely preoccupied with their home and children, a less prestigious occupation they pointed out, feel defensive.

As each side, those who do work and those who don't, becomes defensive, the children in the middle are batted back and forth as proof of the success of one or the other choice. In this perspective the value we place on our children becomes distorted.

Putting children in their place might take on some new meaning. Many working mothers point out that of course we should take children seriously, tend to them, care for them, listen to them, and enjoy them, but they balk at the idea that children should define our adult vision of ourselves. That's oddly inconsistent, they feel, with what most adults want or expect out of life.

Verbal pokes and jabs may seem trivial to some. Critical attitudes toward working mothers are divisive, however, and tend to separate women who ought to be natural allies.

The biggest losers in this opinion war are welfare mothers. In a recent study, a Cornell University professor, Harold Feldman, and his wife, Margaret Feldman, who teaches psychology at Ithaca College, reported that welfare women had "lost control" of their children. "There are negative results from the mother not working," Mrs. Feldman said. Welfare mothers were found to be very "traditional" in their views of the role of women. "Eighty-five per cent said it is more desirable for a woman to stay home than to work. Sixty per cent disagreed that a paid job is more satisfying than being a housewife." At the same time these women wanted to work. "They're in a double bind. Either they go to work (and really hold down two jobs) and get criticized for not taking proper care of their kids, or they don't work to take care of the kids and yet get criticized for being lazy."

In a sample of women in rural West Virginia, Ithaca, New York, and Syracuse, New York, the Feldmans chose families in which half the mothers were working; the other half stayed at home. They found that "the mother's working produced either no effect on the children or a slightly positive effect." Children of working mothers were found to have a slightly higher IQ, but no difference was discernible in their grade point average. The number of days children were absent from school was greater if the mother was at home. Of the children whose mothers worked, 20 per cent had not eaten breakfast, but 30 per cent of those whose mothers did *not* work also had not eaten breakfast.

"All the children, whether their mother was working or not, didn't think it was so bad for their mother to work. But those whose mothers *were* working felt things were going better since they went to work. They were more positive about mothers working."

Mrs. Feldman said that working women clearly think their children are better off as a result, but women who were contemplating work felt their children would suffer if they were employed outside the home.

Alas, the welfare mothers' children suffered the most. "They had the lowest IQs, the lowest grades, watched the most TV, were least likely to value being a good child, were most likely to reject their mothers' values."

The problems of working mothers, I learned, are accentuated by the attitudes most people have regarding the raising of children. Attitudes toward professional fulfillment of women, or so it seemed to the women I talked with, were no where near as highly charged as the assumptions people make over the maternal behavior of mothers who work. Because of this it appears that welfare mothers, and occasionally women in lower status professions, may suffer from a backlash of public opinion—a sneer at women who *choose* to work.

These attitudes toward working mothers might not be so potent if they weren't held by people with powerful influence over mothers and families—doctors, lawyers, teachers, ministers, employers, television personalities, and counselors of all sorts. A woman hardly knows when she starts out to be a working mother how often she will have to confront the convictions of these people. She may blindly thrust herself into a social class discriminated against so subtly that she is unprepared for the blow, simply because she was unaware of the problem. Even when she starts out cheerful, determined, and conscientious in both her jobs, she may end up hostile and hurt.

Much of the psychological stress working mothers have to deal with comes from their perpetual effort to bolster their own convictions. Often the only support they find for their convictions and way of life comes from other working mothers. Then as each group of mothers gravitates to the chosen side, a war rages on.

three

GOING BACK TO WORK: WHEN IS THE BEST TIME?

We decided to have our children close together so that I could spend the first few years at home with them and then go back to work. I wanted to lose as little time as possible and was sure, thanks to everything I read and other women I talked with, that it would be best to be at home for those infant and toddler years. Now our daughters are nearly three and four years old, and six months ago I tried to start work again. It was a disaster. The children simply could not take my long absences. I don't know how other women can do it to their kids. I quit once I saw how much they needed me . . . were used to needing me, probably will continue to need me for years to come. A Twenty-nine-year-old Dental Hygienist/Housewife

Women deciding whether or not to go back to work typically seem to experience a great many agonizing doubts, but there seem to be two periods in a mother's life when that agony seems to be especially prolonged. One period is when the mother has stayed home for just a few years—two to four—and the children are still very young. The other occurs when the children are in early adolescence. These are the two stages in child development when it is most difficult for children to adjust to a new situation. The same periods are proportionately difficult for mothers.

A woman who decides that she wants to go back to work when she has a preschool child has at least two major problems. First, her child has grown to rely on her constant maternal companionship. Her relationship with her baby has grown to be peculiarly intense. Since birth she has been there to answer a dozen needs and provide most of the companionship of life. Only she knows his particular habits and foibles—his eating and sleeping patterns, teddy bear and blanket needs; only she can read the telltale signs that he needs something, is about to get sick, is cutting a tooth, or is afraid of certain noises.

Most mothers know this. Many women admit that they cringe at the notion they could be replaced. How could anyone else provide a mother's care? Witness one more pediatrician on the subject: Mother is the center of a two-year-old's universe. This is why it is ordinarily not a good idea to send a two-year-old to nursery school. Emotionally, he is not ready for it. He is simply not prepared to leave his mother for three hours a day to play with children under the supervision of what to him is a "strange" woman, his teacher. If a working mother has to leave a two-year-old at a day-care center because of economic necessity, then, of course, there is no alternative. But ideally, a child should be three before attending nursery school or a day-care center.*

Psychologists and pediatricians have told us that during the first two or three years of life, and perhaps even more, children need this sort of attentive mothering. So aside from what we've learned from on-the-job training, we are reluctant to think that we *could* be replaced. If it's so easy to replace a child's mother, why stay home in the first place? *So, continuing to stay home becomes a justification for having stayed home.*

This kind of thinking can cloud one's already negligible ability to make decisions about *how* to arrange going back to work.

Children find this period just as difficult. Many preschoolers are trying out nursery schools for the first time. For a three-year-old used to being with his mother all day, this is a big adjustment. Coming home tired and revved up with no mother there to welcome—or control—him is sometimes the final straw.

I asked the director of one large nursery school to study the children who were having a hard time adjusting. Did they have anything in common? The first thing she mentioned was that all these children had unusual tensions at home. About 50 per cent of the troublesome children were from homes where both parents

* Dr. Fitzhugh Dodson, *How to Father*, Nash, 1974.

worked. Of the others, some had mothers anxious to go back to work, or attempting to navigate a transition back to working status. Among working mothers, the tension-producing conflict was a new one, for the most part. A few of the troubled children came from families where husband and wife disagreed about whether or not she should work at all.

All these children were three years old. Several exhibited separation trauma, had difficulty making friends, did not show "leadership" qualities, and were sometimes inhibited in playing out their problems, i.e., dramatizing in their play the conflict they were feeling.

The better-adjusted children of working mothers, by contrast, had lived with the situation since birth. They were used to switching from mother to baby-sitters and playgroups, and had experienced a lot of independent time. They related easily to teachers and other adults associated with the school. When they needed something, they spoke up. When they wanted to play with other children, they went around the classroom and gathered together enough kids to play with them. They managed the transition from indoor to outdoor play relatively easily.

This nursery school director felt that the *mothers* of the children who were having a difficult time were struggling with conflicts between their felt need to fulfill professional ambitions and, at the same time, their need to satisfy childrearing responsibilities. She pointed out that these women were living with two contradictory premises—that they should stay home and that they should get out. Both premises had powerful and articulate advocates, and many women seemed helpless in the face of such unavoidable ambivalence. The children seemed to sense the conflict —and reacted to the *conflict* within the mother, as well as her absence.

Another problem for women with preschoolers who elect to return to work is that they are often hiring household help or baby-sitters for the first time—often with disastrous results. Inexperience, and often a resigned defeatism, seemed the explanation. The process of hiring household help was unfamiliar, they didn't know how to interview, judge resumés, use references, and so on. Many, typically, had been skeptical about being a working mother and, in spite of their decision to join the ranks, clung to the assumption that it was "going to be awfully hard."

The apprehensions felt by these women were often compounded by their husbands, who, noting their wives' anxiety and ambivalence, chimed in with their own doubts. No matter how supportive they might have been when the idea was first mentioned, the wife's decision to go back to work was already proving a source of stress. So they backed off. "Maybe you ought to wait awhile," was the typical response of a husband suddenly alarmed by his new headaches. "Joan thought she would like to go back to work," one husband told me, "but after two months of trying to get good help, she gave up. I told her I liked her at home anyhow. When the children are older it will be easier for her."

When this happens, women are confused. It wasn't supposed to happen, they thought. They had "agreed" to stay home for a couple of years because that is what child experts had suggested. But now they were trapped. What went wrong? Some women, of course, make it through but even they usually find the going rough.

"If I had known how difficult it was going to be to get my son to adjust to a drastic change in my schedule," one mother said, "I never would have quit work when he was born. I've made it through but it will show on him for years, I am sure. With my next child, I'll work right through. I know I want to work, and frankly who doesn't need the money? I was letting my child believe that life was going to be arranged in one way and I knew it wasn't—not forever. I always planned to go back to work, so who was I kidding? Him. They need to get the story straight from the start. In order for me to go back to work when Sam was so young, I either needed exceptional child care, or I had to postpone working until I had finished the job of 'bringing him up.' I saw women who worked right through, and I envied them."

One woman organized a playgroup in her home three mornings a week and hired a college student to run it. But she was fortunate enough to have a large house, with adequate play space, and an extra, tiny apartment to house her live-in student. She hired an older woman in the neighborhood to be on duty when the student had to be away. The situation worked beautifully. Her group included four preschoolers and all were from nearby homes. Her own child never had to make an abrupt adjustment, because she had started the procedure before starting her own job. The adults that came and went with their children were part of an extended family for the child, and of course the prime baby-sitter, the student, was living in the house.

Not everyone can enjoy such a favorable arrangement. Even if they could, many have to deal with their own insecurities about their mothering and, perhaps, some marital adjustment.

"That first year I worked I was really not happy. I was very tense, and had a lot of difficulty learning how to be a mother. We hadn't planned to have children so soon, and had been married for only two years when Rebecca was born. That was a difficult time for me. I ended up going into therapy. I didn't feel comfortable about working, partly because I didn't feel secure in my mothering. Now I feel much different. When I left my Jeb [her one-year-old son] this morning, he reached out for me and said, 'Momma.' I knew that he wanted me to stay home. I felt a pang, but I didn't feel the guilt I felt when Rebecca was two because I have a full feeling of motherliness with Jeb. I don't feel that leaving him is an act of resentment or rebellion against motherhood.

"I know my husband doesn't have any concern about my working now. He thinks it's a really fine thing. We had been very jealous in our affections for one another before, when Rebecca was first born, so the idea of having a three-way relationship was a difficult thing for both of us. We had to learn not just how to *deal* with it but how to *enjoy* it. So that it would be an enhancement of our lives."

Some women who are ambivalent about working when they have preschoolers may need to stay home for a longer period of time. Then, once they feel stronger about it, they may be able to manage the necessary arrangements.

Unfortunately many women don't see things so clearly. Susan, for example, went on to say she didn't feel she could stay home with a clear conscience.

"My working has meant stress for my kids, but if you look at the way it balances out in the whole family system, it has been as good an arrangement as I could hope for. I am not a person who could be satisfied doing child care all day every day, though I think my kids would have preferred it. But I wouldn't have been happy.

"Rebecca had one very difficult time. We had a baby-sitter that she had loved. When the baby-sitter left, Rebecca had a terrific sense of loss. I felt badly about that, that it should never have happened to Rebecca. I should never have allowed her to become so attached to a person who might leave. I felt very guilty. I was pregnant at the time. My husband and I talked a lot then about the pros and cons of my working and my not always being available to Rebecca. At times, I've wished I could have been the kind of person who could stay home and bake bread, do gardening and so forth and not have other ambitions. Or that I could work at home, just go and write. But I *do* need some structure in my life, and I need the company of other working adults. I really can't be in the company of children all day."

Some women were able to go back to work without a ripple of discord. But most of these women had worked long enough before they had children to establish their careers—at least to the point where they could resume them without much trouble. They had more professional self-confidence and enough experience with the working world to know how to prepare for it. Because they hadn't had their babies when they were right out of college, they usually planned them better. They first developed professional skills and professional status. *Then* they had a baby—stayed home for a couple of years before going back to work. Their professional experience prepared them for hiring help, and for making mature judgments without a lot of conflict. One woman, a banker, told me:

"I quit work when I had the baby because I thought it would be good to enjoy some time as a mother for a change. I was twenty-nine and had been working since the day I graduated from college so it seemed time to take a rest. Also, I'd gotten rid of a lot of professional preliminaries.

"I knew I had acquired enough work experience so that I can return at will without losing ground. I'm lucky because my skills are in demand and being a woman has actually been an asset to me on the job. We plan to have one more child soon and I might re-evaluate how long I stay home. But I'll let my mothering and my children pace that for me. In the meantime I enjoy working on a few community things, exploring the museums around here, and getting to know my daughter. Of course it would be nice if my husband could do the same sometime."

She had no conflict about returning to work when she did. Her state of mind was a big asset to her once she did. It's just one less tension she had to deal with. For many women, the additional anxiety over whether they can do a new job well increases their anxiety over leaving the household. Professional self-confidence, of course, is an important ingredient no matter how old a woman is or how old her children are. For women who don't have it, however, or who are trying to go back to work when their child is very young (one to five), their own uneasiness makes it very difficult to handle the preschool demands of their children.

Caroline, an anesthesiologist now practicing in the Southwest, had two children and took off two years for each one. When her first child was born, she was just finishing her first year of internship.

"We had this big decision to make when I was pregnant with Benji. We had not planned to have children until after I had completed my residency and we could afford the kind of help I knew we'd need. My husband was also in residency then, and his schedule was worse than my own. So it was a lousy time to have a baby, if we both continued. On the other hand I had had some gynecological problems and the doctors agreed that I was lucky to be pregnant and might not be able to have another one. So we decided to go through with it, although it was a big blow, to me at least. I had always wanted to go into medicine and had worked very hard getting the best of credentials, putting up with all sorts of chauvinism at Harvard med. school and was frankly mad as hell that I would have to tell my professors I was taking time off for a baby. You should have seen the smiles on their faces.

"Maybe that was why I was so determined. At any rate, I had Benji and took off two years. I would have taken only one but I couldn't get good help that year and both my husband and I felt that without good help we couldn't do it. On our schedules we would both be gone every other night and every other weekend most of the time and sometimes we couldn't co-ordinate our schedules so that we would even be home together in any given week. That, we felt, would really be unfair to the baby."

Caroline knew that she would be going back to work after two years with her baby so she spent much of her time studying. She wanted to be sure that she could pick up where she left off with perfect confidence. She told me that she had always been scornful of doctors who came into the operating room unprepared in the slightest way. Her drive for excellence was strong and one sensed that the years she had stayed home while her husband went off to the hospital might have been frustrating ones. Her "good help" was her mother, whom she imported from Texas to come and live with them. Her son adored his grandmother, something that Caroline felt made up for any in-law problems they had once her mother was established in their household. "I knew I could leave at five-thirty every morning, before Benji woke up, and feel that someone who truly loved him would be there to change him and give him breakfast and coddle him the way mothers and grandmothers do."

Nevertheless, Caroline said it was still hard. If she hadn't been able to meet the standards of her professors and colleagues, she felt, her insecurity in the operating room would have created anxiety for her that she was sure would have rubbed off at home. "Because I was holding up, it made it easier for Benji to do the same." Another source of support for Caroline was her mother's feeling about her career. The neighborhood Caroline lived in was a suburban duplex development filled with young couples and small children. Some of the other mothers of toddlers were also trying to start out at jobs but they did not have Caroline's education or ambitions, although their husbands were young lawyers, doctors, professors, or businessmen. Most wives had terminated their educations with B.A.s or less. She pointed out that no one in their families, least of all their husbands, thought it was very important that they have careers and for the most part their careers were unambitious. These women, she felt, did not have the same kind of support she had. Furthermore, she said, her son, who was left without his parents for much longer periods of time than the other children in the neighborhood, had fewer problems adjusting to life on the sidewalk or in his home. "That made the other women angry, because Benji was a happy little boy and, once the initial period was over, adjusted just beautifully. I still think it was because I felt no conflict over what I was doing. I enjoyed him when I was with him and he knew it."

A strong factor in this confidence, Caroline thought, was that her decision to have him, and her mothering, were not escapes from her profession, and her profession was not an escape from him. "I always loved coming home to them and I never felt guilty much, when I had to leave. My sons didn't see me agonize."

In general, women who go back to work after two or three years have nowhere near this kind of support or conviction. Support and conviction are hard to come by at any stage, but they are much more needed with younger children, who are less able to comprehend what is happening and their schedules and needs are more complex than older children's. Also, they feel the mother's conflict and insecurities.

Women who wait until the youngest child goes to first grade seem to have the easiest time. Going back to work when children are between the ages of six and eleven seems to be relatively easy for everyone. School hours are longer, ranging from 8 A.M. to 2 or 4 P.M. More important, children at this age frequently are more preoccupied with their own lives than with their parents'. On the whole, their weekdays are absorbed with activities involving friends in the neighborhood or other independent involvements. When they come home from school, elementary schoolers rush in, change their clothes, and rush out again. They roller skate, play ball games, take lessons, join clubs, visit other kids' homes, ride bikes, and do a hundred things that don't require constant maternal attention.

Grade school children are more able to talk about and understand where their mother is going, what it means to her, and sometimes to feel an inkling of pride in their mother's work. They aren't afraid to be left alone for an hour or two (3 P.M. to 5 P.M. if necessary), especially not the child who is eight years old or over. In fact they enjoy their independence. They are at a more secure age and therefore more adaptable.

Of course the post 5 P.M. supper hour may prove to be a difficult period for these mothers, chiefly because they have additional chores to do before they can relax, and because children save up their talk about school and other important developments for the moment she walks in the door. As one woman said, "I never know which one is needing an ear the most. They all wave their papers in my face and talk at the same time. It's a crazy welcome. But we get used to it."

It isn't that these mothers have to worry less about the development of their children or pay less attention to their schooling, but that the children are at a very outgoing, involved period of life. They aren't so threatened; they aren't so worried about things they can't express or understand. Some mothers told me they could see this period coming on when their children were five. Five, according to Gesell, is the easiest period anyway. "Five years of age marks, in many children, a time of extreme and delightful equilibrium," writes Gesell. "The five year old tends to be reliable, stable, well adjusted. Secure within himself, he is calm, friendly, and not too demanding in his relations with others." If it weren't for the problem of brief kindergarten hours, the five-year-old plateau is probably just as good a starting-off point for mothers returning to work as the time when children enter first grade.

Conventional wisdom on these matters, however, is not widely shared or understood. One psychologist, who had read extensively about mothering and children's development, told me, "I was misled. Everything I read told me to stay home for the first two years *at least*. That implied that after two years, I could go out and work with a relatively free conscience. It just isn't so. If they had told me from the start, 'Look, you've got to stay home for five to six years,' I would have obeyed. And I would have had it easier and so would my children. But it was difficult and stressful to go back after two years. I thought we were an aberration. I hadn't done it right. Everything was a mess. I had five housekeepers in one year. Everything went wrong. My son wouldn't toilet train; his diet is rather bizarre; he has a hard time going to sleep at night; he has a hard time making friends. The list is endless. I think it's just the worst time for a mother to go back to work."

Another mother, who waited until her youngest was six, said, "I don't think I had many problems. Jessy was in the first grade and the other kids were older. In fact, if you want to know the truth, I sometimes felt I wasn't missed. I was tired a lot but I seemed to be able to hold up until after supper and I never felt bad about asking the children to help out. Our suppertimes were pretty good. My husband and I felt it was important for us to eat together, so he got home as early as he could. I'm not saying it wasn't hard, but it didn't seem to be so hard on *them*. They probably liked the fact that I wasn't around so much. I got off their backs. You know, the big snoop, she went back to work, thank God."

However, if a woman waits too long, she can hit another troubled time and her efforts to get back to work will meet opposition. Children in early adolescence are more demanding, more apprehensive, and more easily perturbed. Yet women have also been led to believe this is a good time to start work. Children in their *early* adolescence may *seem* to be more grown up than they are, even though they crave more and more independence. Certainly they *want* personal responsibilities, like buying their own clothes, earning their own money, having time to themselves that is not always accounted for. Many, on the other hand, need help in handling their new responsibilities, especially if they're not used to assuming so many.

Young teen-agers are deciding about many things and trying out a lot of new behavior and experiences. After ten, they cease to believe automatically that their parents are reliable authorities on any subject. So it's not, as one woman put it, that the children need to have a mother around to ask permission for a lot of things or be watched over all the time for their own safety. They do need, whether or not they are willing to admit it, a certain kind of *availability*.

These kids want to form their own opinions. They don't want to be told nor are they willing to accept parental judgments on all things. Even so, they also need and like to talk about things with their parents.

Madeline had brought up five children, and had worked for short times over the course of their childhoods. She told me:

"All my kids are different. Some are talkers and some aren't, but you have to watch out for both kinds. They're thinking all the time. Most kids in grade school will gab on and on about the things that happen in school and it's all off the top of their heads. Often you can get by with a commiserating remark. But starting in junior high, things change. They're thinking about things in a much more serious way and it's not so easy to pull it out in the the evening with parents and other siblings around. But, boy, I've learned this: They need to talk. They've got a lot sitting inside them. And they don't always take to the old ways of bringing it out. What's really bothering them may not come out at the dinner table. And you càn't just sit down and say, 'Let's have a talk,' and expect the kid to loosen up."

Madeline felt strongly that it was necessary to make time available so that children of this age could ease themselves into certain conversations. If every day, day after day, a woman provides only one hour after supper to be with her children, "not much can happen," she felt. "I got so I could sense when something was going to come out of one of them, and I found I had to prolong whatever it was that I was doing in the kitchen way beyond what I needed in order to do what I was doing so that the child could get at it without letting me know, almost, that she was talking about it at all. This is because what they really want to do is make up their own minds. At the same time, they want to find out what you think or they want to talk about it without the fear that you will jump in and tell them what has to be done, or what they ought to think or do." Children, she had found, might talk at length about all the sexual activity that other kids were involved in and never mention themselves. "So you have to be careful not to push them into anything they're not prepared for."

Madeline was aware of a need for some flexibility in her life in order to be there when her children might need her, to give them a chance to talk to her without making it a big deal. "In our family we all have times and ways we get into these discussions. Everything has evolved into the way we keep up with each other. When the kids were younger, my husband and I could pretty much set the pace. But by the time they turned eleven or twelve, things changed. The kids wanted to take a bigger role in determining our family time. They will accept things that have always been—for instance, supper at six or having friends in, as we often do, on Sunday afternoons. But they don't like us to impose on them during the week. They're busy filling up their time with their own new things."

Madeline concluded that it was a bad idea to try to change things drastically in a family during these early adolescent years. She had experience with both ways in her family. For her first two children she had worked continuously. But when her third child was in the fifth through the seventh grade, she had to stay home and nurse a bad back. As soon as she was better, she went right back to work. "Whammo. My son started having problems in school. He was having a rough time and he didn't seem to be able to find me, you know, in the abstract sense. We finally found a guidance counselor at the school who would work with us but I learned a lesson. You can't take much for granted, at least not with kids."

Madeline was not talking about scheduled blocks of time when she spoke of "availability." With five children and a busy household she probably never had a lot of time. But there are times and there are times. "Availability" can mean psychic availability, being aware of things, not being so preoccupied you're not truly there.

Another woman, Pat, had a similar problem with her thirteen-year-old daughter.

"Sally always used to come and talk with me while I was making supper. I like to cook and we always had a good hour to relax in the kitchen. When I went back to work, I didn't have that hour any more. I'd get through at five, rush to a grocery store on the way home, and then get in the house in time to throw something together, use a lot of convenience foods, and empty the breakfast dishes from the dishwasher just in time for my husband to arrive. Then everyone converged on the kitchen. I could see that Sally sometimes missed the time we had together and so I would try to make it up later in the night. I'd suggest that we make some brownies or that she'd join me in my bedroom when I sorted the family laundry or something. But it wasn't the same. In the first place Sally often had other things to do later on in the evening or there would be a television program the whole family wanted to watch or we were all tired. If you ask me what I had to give up when I went back to work, I'd say it was that—my talks with Sally. She's my only daughter and, you know, that's a lot to give up."

Some women found that early adolescent children had anxieties no one had anticipated. And, to make matters worse, many mothers discovered new anxieties in themselves. They were measuring themselves against other women at their place of work. They were worried they had forgotten too much. They were trying to prove they could do the job well. They were dealing with fatigue they hadn't felt in years. When they got home they had lots of things to talk about with their husbands, and that cut into family time. Some women said they were aware of a temporary self-centeredness, even selfishness, that they knew was not natural for them.

"Kids tense up anyway, during this early teens period, and that makes parents tighter than usual—just in the way they approach each other," one woman said. "So when I got anxious about my new job, that just threw more fat on the fire."

One father, admittedly from the "old school," saw it from a slightly different perspective. "Look, these kids today come home from school in the middle of the afternoon and trouble is waiting for them on every corner. I don't care what you say, they need their mother home to see that they stay out of it. How do you

know what your kid's been doing when you're off takin' a coffee
break with the girls at the office? If you're not there, you just
won't know, and I see it happening every day and right here on
this street."

His wife added, "I know what he means, though I think my
kids know what's expected of them. But you do worry more. I
never worried when they were younger, and we had a baby-sitter,
but they're too old for a baby-sitter now. I have them call me
when they get home and I try to sense if anything is going on."

The women who had the hardest times went back to work
without understanding that it was going to be difficult. The
switch seems particularly hard for women with many children.
For those families with kids spaced widely enough so that it is
practically impossible to find a time when they are all in the same
stage together, it may be necessary to pay particular attention to
whatever child is developmentally out of sorts. These experiences
seem to suggest some conclusions.

First, that the easiest times for a mother to return to work are:
1) when her baby is still an infant (and can adapt to the schedule
of two working parents immediately and without conscious
stress); or 2) once her child has reached elementary school, and
no longer expects intensive around-the-clock attention.

The most difficult times to return to work seem to be: 1) when
children are in the preschool stage, before the age of five, and easily upset by sudden changes in their mothers' schedule; and 2)
when children are in *early* adolescence, struggling with ambivalence over parental authority and an impulse toward independence, and needing, at the same time, a secure parental situation.

four

WHAT WILL HAPPEN TO
THE CHILDREN?

The great majority of published writing about effects of maternal employment on children has taken a markedly negative stance: assuming that maternal employment must be harmful for children, the investigators have often phrased hypotheses, and questionnaires, so that only ill effects can be demonstrated. One begins his report, "The writer has long cherished the opinion that the employment of mothers in occupations outside their homes is a potent factor in producing maladjustment among the children of those mothers." While it is of inestimable assistance to the reader to have such bias honestly displayed, one searches in vain for serious efforts to investigate the opposed position. MARY C. HOWELL, "Effects of Maternal Employment on the Child," *Pediatrics*, Vol. 52, No. 3, September 1973*

The strongest fear inherent in the working-mother situation is that the children will suffer from parental neglect. Some women remark, "I feel that if I'm going to have children, I ought to stay home and take care of them." "Will these be my children, or a housekeeper's children?" others argue. Or, "I feel that if you give them a strong, close beginning, a good one-to-one mother-child relationship they can count on, then you've put them on the right road. Maybe then you can be gone more from the house."

Many experts argue that the first few years of a child's life require the kind of constant care that only a nonworking mother can give. One widely read pediatrician even cautions mothers who want to leave their child for a few hours each day.

> It's important to feel free enough to go shopping, visit friends, and handle similar matters away from home. But don't overdo it. The point I want to make is that your baby becomes attached to you and misses you when you are not there. Some babies, cared for by others from the start, don't attach themselves strongly enough to their parents to care whether the parents are or are not with them. While this might be convenient for a mother who wants more "freedom," she is in a sense preventing her child from establishing a close tie to his mother.*

Women who read those words are apt to worry that they may be pushing things by leaving their baby longer than it takes to go to the supermarket. "Babies cared for by others from the start" will echo in their ears as they contemplate taking a job or keeping a job after having a baby. No mother wants to relinquish a "close tie" to her child, and the suggestion here is that she probably will —if she leaves him for a job, she throws him into the arms of some mother substitute.

How real should such fears be? What demands can a mother make on her child? What are the consequences of working motherhood on the child? The working mothers I talked to about this tended to break these questions down into periods of the child's life.

INFANTS AND BABIES

Many women said that the period when they first went back to work after childbirth was harder on them than it was on their babies. *Mothers* felt separation pangs. *They* wondered if they were doing the right thing. Sometimes they wished they could have it both ways—stay home longer but also return to work. They were often tired all the time. Some experienced ambivalence toward the people they were working with. More often than not they felt isolated from the rest of the world, misunderstood, and

* Dr. Lee Salk, *What Every Child Would Like His Parents to Know*, McKay, 1972.

too preoccupied with their new baby and their various jobs to pay attention to much else.

But this fear on the part of working mothers that they'll be replaced in their baby's eyes doesn't seem based on fact. In a recent book authored by two men, both fathers, one a psychologist at the University of Rhode Island, the other a science writer for MIT, the point is made that their research indicates that the children of working mothers are as a group similar to children of nonworking mothers in terms of emotional, intellectual, and physical development.

> Such children show as much attachment to their mothers as children of mothers who are housewives. This is mainly because the mother who goes off to work every day is likely to realize that her children definitely need a period of playing with her and being with her when she gets home, and she allows for this. In fact, the child may get even more out of the working Mom than out of the housewife Mom, who may not really feel the need to interact as positively with her child. After all, she may feel, she is always at home anyway. . . .†

Also, more than half of the two hundred or so women I interviewed had gone back to work within three months after having their babies, and all felt their children had developed a strong relationship with them. No woman felt that a baby-sitter or some other surrogate had replaced her in her child's affections.

Many women are able to get home for an hour at noon to feed, often nurse, their babies. But whether or not they can do that, they say they usually find a peaceful child when they do get home. "Leaving my baby when he was an infant was easier on *me* than leaving him later on would be," many women told me. "Once he is old enough to sit up, grin, fuss, or hold his hands out for a pick-up, then a different kind of wrench sets in."

Most women admitted that their babies obviously would prefer it if they stayed home, even though a baby may adjust fairly well to the daily morning separation. But as one woman put it, "My baby would also rather eat animal crackers all day long. That doesn't mean I let him. I try to offer him a variety of foods just as I try to offer him a variety of experiences. My comings and goings, routine as they are, are accepted by him now just the way the

† BILLER and MEREDITH, *Father Power*, McKay, 1975.

spinach in his warming dish has come to be tolerated. Not that he doesn't spit the spinach out a lot—but I wouldn't like it if he didn't balk at my leaving him once in a while. It's a sign to me that he does care for me."

Many women reported that at first they had worried that their babies would establish too strong a tie with a baby-sitter, but the women who lived through this period said they often laughed at their fears later. "The best thing I ever did for my children," one forty-two-year-old woman told me, "was get them used to other adults at an early age. My kids still know who's mother and father, and who loves and cares for them all the time. How could there be any doubt about it? The suggestion that some hired person, I don't care how loving or careful, could replace that sense of family seems to me short-sighted. What's a few hours away from a child each day compared to the years and nights and weekends and every other moment you spend with them? You share much more as a family than any nurse, baby-sitter or guardian of any sort could."

Another young mother told me, "I think Dr. Spock places too high a value on *tradition*, doing things the way grammy did. Some 'grammys' were perfect fools, as are, of course, some mothers. Whatever the case, I think we, I, need to make sense of the process ourselves, on the basis of reason, not ritual."

Some working mothers discover that the demands they put on their children in infancy—the daily separation—encourage a sense of trust in the mother's eventual reappearance. This sense of trust seems to develop most quickly when women leave for their jobs in a confident manner, return promptly at the same time each day, and when other members of the family support with the same confidence the mother's decision to work. Once a pattern of comings and goings has been established and the household is running smoothly on all other fronts, the joy of a new infant and the intimate parental relations that are part of that joy come naturally and without difficulty to many working mothers.

The consensus of these working mothers is that leaving an infant forty hours a week in order to work won't, in and of itself, disturb the relationship between mother and child. Or father and child. Plenty of time and ways remain to establish a strong maternal tie, to nurse if a woman wishes, to enjoy the development of a baby's first years. Most women also agree that an important ingredient in settling an infant into a working mother's schedule is consistency, a strict routine that involves prompt comings and goings of both parents—so that an infant can rely on the reappearance of both parents each day when he has come to expect it. Consistency in all child care is crucial. If an infant is put into an institutional infant-care program, the program should be small, with the same adults in charge of it at the same time each day. If at-home care is used, the same person should be there each day and should be reliable enough so that both parent and child can count on it.

One woman, who had been a day-care teacher for five years, and is herself the mother of a two and a half-year-old boy, scoffed at the notion that children who had been at the center full time since they were three months old had difficulty associating with their parents. "We teachers talk about this fear parents seem to have and we wonder at it. It is so obvious to us that we could never replace any mother or father. One visible proof of this is the way, when the chips are down, a small child will *always* cry for his or her mother or father. This in spite of the fact that the child has spent full days with us since birth."

Many women feel that the tug they felt in leaving an infant to go off to work is "conditioned." Understanding what are conditioned and what are natural feelings may be very difficult for women who have been brought up to believe in the Johnson's baby powder version of infant care—the kind that many women envisioned for themselves. That life with an infant, in particular one's own, would consist of sweet moments with a cherubic baby who needed a mother there at every waking moment.

Many women I talked with pointed out that this image of blissful and constant maternal care of infants is romanticized. Not only do infants sleep a lot during the time a mother is supposed to busy herself about the house, but even when they are awake they are often exploring a world larger than a mother's lap. Guidance in their discoveries is certainly needed. But that sort of guidance, these mothers have observed, can easily come from other adults without jeopardizing the relationship with the mother.

Many of the women I talked with observed that many of their ideas about infant care were traceable to the advertising by baby food companies, powder and diaper businesses, and to magazine articles they'd read in the offices of gynecologists. Counteracting this stream of visionary expectations were rare encounters with real live infants, especially infants as tiny as the ones they brought home from the hospital.

Once they did get home from the hospital, these women found that they had to alter their image of their role, their infants' needs, their own needs. If they were determined to be working women, they had to examine their natural feelings and needs to decide what was feasible and what was not. Many of these women discovered they were not capable of maintaining a constant vigil over the crib. Their maternal behavior was affected by the amount of time they had away from their babies. Many felt guilty. Others felt relieved once they saw that this was natural and, in many cases, preferable. Some recent research supports their view.

> Professional child caretakers observe that approximately six hours per day is the maximum amount of time most inter- ested and able adults can invest in meaningful interaction with children. Full-time homemaker-mothers report that they spend, on the average, six-plus hours in child care, when they have more than one child, compared to employed mothers who spend four-plus hours in child care. It has been estimated that the difference in "attentive" care is probably not signifi- cant.‡

One woman who had returned to work when her first baby was seven weeks old described her relatively guilt-free experiences. "I feel my life with our baby is more clean-cut than that of some other mothers I know," she said. "There are definite times when I'm away from him and then when I am with him, I am *really* with him. If I were home all day, there would be times during the day that, although I would be in the house, I would have to be unavailable to the baby—simply because I would have other things to do and because I couldn't stand not to have some time to myself. This way my time with my child is structured without the struggle housewives feel they have with their children—the struggle to get away, to maintain a high level of child interest all day.

One woman told me her pediatrician had warned her not to overcompensate for her absences in such a way that she made the

‡ Mary C. Howell, "Employed Mothers and Their Families," *Pediatrics*, Vol. 52, No. 2, August 1973.

baby depend on her too much. He told her that women who work often insist on a very dependent tie with their baby when they return, and on weekends. This tendency, he told her, was usually the result of deep-seated maternal guilt. "If you feel confident about working," he said, "then chances are your baby will too."

PRESCHOOLERS AND OLDER CHILDREN

Not all women, of course, discover immediately how important it is for the child to sense that his mother is confident about working. Eva, for example, found it difficult to work and leave her small children. She had worked off and on part time since her children were born, but mostly she had been at home during the day and had juggled her work to meet their schedules. When her youngest was three, she decided to go to law school, full time. During her first year of classes, Eva's youngest son, Carl, developed separation problems at nursery school. He balked at leaving home in the morning, lost his appetite, cried when the baby-sitter picked him up, and was irritable during school hours. Naturally Eva was upset. And naturally she attributed her son's difficulties to her new schedule. She tried soothing him, lingering at the nursery school in the mornings to reassure him. She spent intense loving moments with him when she got home at the end of the day. But Carl's resistance only intensified.

One evening Eva's husband pointed out that she was always apologizing to Carl about her working. "You never see me apologizing about going off to work in the morning, and Carl trusts *me*. He doesn't cry when I go."

Eva was astonished, and for a time, angry. She found it difficult to believe that she might be to blame for her son's opposition to the new schedule. She had assumed it was the *fact* of her working that caused the problem. But she soon realized that she'd been reluctant to relinquish any of her maternal role. During Carl's peevishness, her husband had come home at odd hours of the day to help out while Eva was attending classes. She realized she was actually undercutting his attempts to be a parent by suggesting to her son that only his mother was sad to leave. She had never once told her son, "Today is daddy's day to be here at noon, I'll be here later," and expect him to accept the change. In both her manner and speech she had implied that Carl would just have to put up with daddy until the more desirable parent got home.

Once Eva understood what she was doing, she stopped apologizing and simply went to her classes. Before long, Carl adjusted to his new circumstances.

Eva had to learn to trust that her child would still love her; and he had to learn that she was not deserting him. As she put it, "Our love for each other was not made up of car pools, lunches, any rainy afternoons in the house. It was made of a kind of absolute assurance we both felt that no matter where we both were, we trusted that we were still important to each other. Now I understand that and can teach it to him."

Feeling secure in the pattern of life, and learning to trust in parental affection are two separate basics that working mothers need to sort out for their children. But it is easy to confuse them. Once again pediatric literature isn't a reliable contemporary source of comfort. In his revised and enlarged edition of *Baby and Child Care*, Dr. Benjamin Spock has this to say about women returning to work:

> The important thing for a mother to realize is that the younger the child, the more necessary it is for him to have a steady, loving person taking care of him. In most cases, the mother is the best one to give him this feeling of "belonging," safely and surely. She doesn't quit on the job, she takes care of him always in the same familiar house. If a mother realizes clearly how vital this kind of care is to a small child, it may make it easier for her to decide that the extra money she might earn, or the satisfaction she might receive from an outside job, is not so important after all.*

The implication here is that alternatives to around-the-clock mothering are grim, though on the whole Spock addresses these remarks to women who *have a choice*. An earlier passage in the same book: "Some mothers *have* to work to make a living. Usually their children turn out all right, because some reasonably good arrangement is made for their care."†

Spock goes on to say that many poor children are neglected and maladjusted, and that the government should assist these families.

* Pp. 563–64; Pocket Books.
† Ibid., p. 563.

Even so, he says reassuringly, most of the poor children of working mothers "turn out all right." And of course they do. It seems
likely, then, that those who *have* a choice might learn from those
who do not.

How is it that many poor children grow up happy and secure in
their familial affections? Why, if these children "turn out all
right," does it follow that middle-class women do a better job by
staying home? And, how do poor women manage to do a good job
of mothering? My interviews suggest at least a few answers.

First, women who work to support a family have the support,
psychologically, of society. Not that government or industry does
the job it ought to; but people sympathize, automatically, with a
mother who has five children and is working full time in a factory.
Not so with a woman earning $25,000 a year, with four children, a
full-time housekeeper, and a husband earning $40,000 a year. The
world shakes its head at that.

Women in factories are not made to feel guilty about their
jobs. If anything, public attitudes favor full-time employment for
mothers, even of small children—if the alternative is adding the
mother's name to the welfare rolls. So *poor* working women are
encouraged to feel they are doing the right thing. Once they lose
any feeling of conflict over whether or not they ought to work,
women are able to attack their dual role with more confidence
than, for example, Eva found possible at first.

Second, and perhaps more important, these women have the
support of their families. Most of the working-class women I met
lived close to other family members and could call upon them for
help. Many of them used grandmothers, sisters, and aunts for
child care. Work, for these women, was part of a team effort and
everyone recognized the necessity of pitching in. This rubbed off
on their children as they too grew old enough to help. Many of
these children, and their parents, had learned from past generations that, in order to survive, family members had to help each
other.

Working-class women I talked with pointed out that they were
also supported by friends on the job—more so than middle-class
women I talked with, who tended to isolate their private and career relationships (many said they were concerned that their husbands "won't like" friends they've made at work). Factory
workers met many other women on the job who were also

mothers and they did not feel isolated, unusual, or required to prove that they could manage motherhood and the job as well. Many middle-class women, in contrast, felt that they were in the minority in their offices, and had few other working mothers to associate with. Not so with the women I met in factories. They called on their friends to help them out in emergencies, to cover for them when family demands required their absence, and to become virtually a part of their home lives.

Finally, working-class mothers were bolstered psychologically by the encouragement of professional people with whom they came in contact—doctors, pediatricians, clergy, teachers, and social workers.

This support system helped working-class mothers avoid agonizing over whether or not they should be away from their home and children. Mary, thirty-five years old, had been working at various factory jobs for fifteen years. When I met her she was working forty hours a week and her youngest was six years old . . . her oldest fourteen. She had used a variety of baby-sitting arrangements through the years—her mother, her sister, her husband's sister—and for a while she brought her daughter to the house of a woman with her own children. "That was fine for the baby, but it was rough on me. But my daughter, on the other hand, was more outgoing, less shy. It sounds crazy, but better adjusted really. I think it was good for her to be around all sorts of people. I left my oldest and youngest child right away to go back to work. These two I get along fine with. The second child, though, was a sickly baby. She was a more demanding child . . . expected more. She was selfish. I've had a hard time with her. Just now it is starting to change. I may have been making demands on those other two, but they're better off for it. Much more independent."

One reason working-class women seem more comfortable teaching their children to be independent may be that they have had to learn to be independent themselves. They have not always had the support of husbands. Although working-class women get lots of female support from their extended family, their husbands tend to remain aloof from child care, claiming they're not going to do "women's work." Women like Mary, as a consequence, wind up raising the children alone, a task they take seriously and realistically. They know how much their children have to learn to stand on their own two feet. Mary realized this when her first two children were toddlers:

"My husband and I get home around 6:30 or 7 P.M. The three kids all want to talk at once. He, my husband, goes into the parlor, flips on the TV, and sits down. It kills me, but that's the way he is. I had told him a long time ago, when the kids were little, and he started finding odd jobs to do, if he doesn't want to be around while they're little, 'When they're teen-agers,' I said, 'don't think you're going to step in. If you don't want to be a father until they're sixteen, I'm sorry. You're not going to start then.'

"I reminded him of that last night 'cause he had started in with the oldest one. And I told him, 'Do you remember back when? Now she's almost fifteen, she's got a life of her own. She's what she's gonna be. There's nothing you can do now about it. You had to be there when she was growin' up.'

"So he calls me 'the mouth.'"

Through the years Mary asked her daughters to assume much of the burden of running the household—but not too much. She pointed out that she felt it was wrong to rob children of the fun of being young. Nevertheless, she felt strongly that they ought to know who paid for things in life and that they would have to assume some responsibility for the welfare of their family. She began teaching them this when they were babies, teaching them in a very practical way—not just "to play house," but to understand that things had to get done.

"I started getting the girls to help around the house when they were real little—two years old. They'd help me make a bed. And they all had an interest in cooking. When you got a little two-year-old begging to help there at the stove, your nerves are raw, but you have to give her something to do. I'd start them out on little things like pudding, scrambled eggs, a can of soup, applesauce. I'd let them peel an apple, just one little apple with tiny little peels. Little things. If I was cookin' supper, I'd let them help me. This is what I was trying to explain to my husband. This goes with it."

Mary was full of stories about her children. She was so proud of them she sometimes had to check herself in embarrassment. While we were talking, her three daughters came home from school and spent a few moments with us before going out to play.

They talked into my tape recorder and showed us their papers and then went off to change their clothes. They were beautiful children, vivacious, curious, and accepting. I understood why Mary was so proud of them.

Many women lack Mary's confidence—at least until they have several years of experience behind them. Once they have learned to insist that their children adjust to their schedules, to the necessity for early independence and serious responsibilities, they find their anxieties over the demands they have to make on their children are based on myth, not reality and experience.

What is the source of that myth? Here is Dr. Salk, in his book *Preparing for Parenthood*, on working mothers: "I have no objections whatsoever to working mothers or, for that matter, to working fathers provided that the little children they have chosen to bring into this world do not suffer." But only one kind of care, in his view, is a safeguard against that kind of suffering. Parents (mothers), he says, should not leave their babies for more than three or at the most four hours a day and once a child is ready for school parents should plan to be at home when the child returns. "A child whose working parents treat him with benign neglect soon learns the best way to demand their interest. If he is paid attention to only when he is ill, he soon uses physical complaints to get his busy parents' recognition. Sometimes being destructive does the trick, or getting into trouble at school."

Working mothers, ironically, seem to spend more time with their children on their off hours—evenings and weekends—than nonworking mothers do. Working mothers, for instance, are apt to keep their children up later in the evening in order to spend time with them. Nonworking mothers are apt to put their children to bed early, have them nap more, and/or use child care at odd hours to give them some time for their own pursuits. Working mothers, on the other hand, rarely use baby-sitters in the evening on weekdays and spend weekend time with their children more conscientiously than nonworking mothers feel the need to. The working mothers I spoke to found it relatively easy to adjust their infants' schedules so that his or her longest wakeful period was during the supper and early evening time, something most nonworking mothers strive to avoid. In this way the working mother had a longer day for a few months but found the solution worth the effort. As one woman put it:

"I stayed home with my first child and I always tried to get the baby to bed before I even ate my supper with my husband. He hardly ever saw the baby. This time we both come home and play with him while we eat and have a drink and then let him stay up practically until we're ready for bed. We discovered since we started this routine that the baby sleeps through the night more often, and my husband feels more a part of the relationship. Once in a while I get tired and wish I had some quiet private time, but this won't last forever. Babies are only infants for a few months so it's not as if it were that much of an imposition."

My research indicates that working mothers, on the whole, work extraordinarily hard to compensate for their time away from home and conscientiously try to give their children a lot of attention when they *are* home. They do not feel, as a body, that their children are neglected or feel neglected. Their children did not exhibit the symptoms of child neglect that Salk describes—illnesses, withdrawal, misbehavior.

These children had learned to adapt somewhat to the *parents'* hours, responding to a fundamental demand put on them from birth. Nonworking mothers usually adapt to the *children's* schedules. Salk and Spock might argue that adults should do the adjusting, since they are more mature and better able to understand and control their feelings. Perhaps. The fact remains, however, that many children *have* adjusted, seem to accept the change without unhappiness, and often thrive in the midst of precisely the sort of arrangement Spock and Salk plainly fear and distrust.

Whenever this issue is discussed in pediatric literature it is phrased in dramatic either/or language.

Salk, in *Preparing for Parenthood*, tells a terrible story of two working parents and their misbehaving child. The parents sound like monsters, unmoved by their child's obvious emotional needs and absurdly impressed with themselves and their careers—too busy, says Salk indignantly, to arrange a conference to discuss their child's problems. This is the *only* example of working parents described in the chapter of his book devoted to "A Life of Your Own Away from Your Baby." This kind of pediatric literature, guaranteed to be on every reading list of every childbirth class in America, intimidates parents who don't know better, and seems certain to cause family stress.

Women who haven't felt any pressure on this issue, I found,

quite naturally struck a balance between what they asked of themselves in the way of adjustments and what they asked of their babies. One woman, Erica, had her first baby when she was thirty-two. She was an independent woman, had worked at a prestigious job for ten years, and had married when she was thirty. She seemed less vulnerable to other people's criticism than many younger women, and her relationship with her baby had been a satisfying one.

"I thought I was going to be reluctant to give up any of my maternal role. I thought, what is it going to be like when Franco, our baby, falls and goes running to our baby-sitter, Joanne, instead of me. Sometimes he goes to Joanne, sometimes to me. I don't know why but he relies on her for certain things and he relies on me for things that are very important to me. He has his own relationship with me. We're three different people, Franco, Joanne, and myself. He'll ask me, when she's there, for something to drink or something to eat or whatever, so he doesn't think of her only in that way. There's no separation there. I don't think I feel any pangs of jealousy about his relationship with her. That makes it easier for me."

It may help confused working mothers to note that many published arguments for not working during a child's infancy come from studies in progress on animal (not human) behavior. Chimpanzees, monkeys, and other mammals, it can be shown, need a close *maternal* one-to-one relationship during their infancy and early childhood. Maternal rejection in animals—meaning behavior in mother animals which, to many people, parallels human maternal behavior typical of the working mother demands—produces neurotic animals unable to survive the rigors of jungle or wild life. These poor baby animals struggle alone, never gain a strong sense of their personal security, and tackle everyday survival problems without an aggressive surety in their ability to survive.

These studies may be quite accurate and certainly interesting—to our understanding of animal behavior. Zoos should take note.

But human mothers and fathers ought to think about some important distinctions. I can think of two that appear, to me, to be pertinent. First, most animal fathers, to my knowledge, count for little in this arrangement of parental roles. Human fathers, on the other hand, are capable of offering important support and understanding to parental obligations and rewards. Human fathers can, in fact, take care of children without any mothers at all. And in a crunch they do.

Second, humans, unlike their animal friends, can learn about and hire good child care for their offspring that, if carefully chosen and trained, can offer considerable support, provide a range of cognitive development programs, and offer security, love, and even fun to babies and preschoolers.

WHAT ARE THE CONSEQUENCES?

Although leaving babies to go off to work seems to be the most controversial demand working mothers make on children, women with older children often feel the problems are compounded with each stage of development. The children of working mothers often have to wait until the end of the day for maternal solace. Most mothers arrange for housekeepers or baby-sitters to be at home when school-aged children get home, but some can't arrange even that. Neighbors are often asked to be on the lookout. Most women have their children call them as soon as they get home, and almost all structure the time their children have alone so that they will be busy and purposeful. Children are expected to do their homework first or some household chore. Many have lessons or group activities in the afternoon that keep them preoccupied. Whatever the solution, not one woman I talked to thought of this period as insignificant.

As mother and child are able to step back and lead lives with greater independence from each other, working mothers often establish an unusually objective view of their children's development. This objectivity may be the result of being told more about their children—through the reports of baby-sitters, day-care teachers, and the like—than nonworking mothers often are. They seem to have additional sources for feedback based on close contact with the child. They also have an unusual viewing stance—their place of work—in order to mull over what is happening with their children before they decide what to do about it.

Many nonworking mothers, for instance, who are continually exposed to their child's misbehavior, react quickly and swiftly without time or energy for reflection. Dr. Spock (*Raising Children in a Difficult Time*) encourages this kind of mothering. "For the natural and easy way to raise children is the same way you were raised yourself: then you don't have to stop and think about what is right and best." This advice is fine for mothers who had a good relationship with their own parents, but what of all the women in the world who vow not to visit the sins of their parents on their own children?

Working mothers often feel less prone to "look the other way" when they shouldn't, to react irrationally to a child's natural demands, and to forget their own resolutions. They are tired a lot, they say, but they're not tired of children, least of all their own. They're tired of the rest of the world or just worn down physically. Somehow, however, they seem to be able to put out for their kids. Many housewives, women point out, simply exhausted from taking care of children all day, perk up when husbands offer to take them out to dinner or a party in the evening. They find that although they were aching for bed at five, they are able to carry on with adults in the evening for another six or seven hours. Reverse the situation and the case of working mothers is easier to understand.

One woman who had just returned to work told me she was prepared to give extra attention to her three-year-old since she had placed him in a day-care center.

She pointed out that, when she picked up her son at the end of her workday, he was exhausted and his behavior was difficult. She had been forewarned that it would take some time for her son to adjust to the long hours of stimulation at a day-care center. Even she marveled at her ability to respond tenderly to his demands. "Danny was so tired he would often burst into tears if he dropped his fork at the dinner table. I would sit with him, even hold him in my lap and feed him. Ordinarily I would have resented giving that kind of attention so late in the day. I was tired too. Blissfully so. *But I wasn't tired of him.* I had whole pounds of mothering inside me anxious to be drawn on."

Another woman told me that her children provided a kind of "moistening" in her day-to-day life. If her life, which consisted of teaching English literature to college students, was made of only work, it would be cold and dry, she said. Her family kept her enriched.

Many working mothers told me they felt more *consciously* aware of their children's ups and downs, their problems, successes, happiness, and sadness. They kept a better watch.

I couldn't help noticing a certain analytical view that working mothers had about their children's development. They were extremely articulate, and like most mothers, they took their children's lives seriously. But they seemed to have an added objectivity which seemed healthy.

One woman who had stayed home with two children for six years and then took a full-time job in a bank told me:

"I no longer needed my children to fulfill every aspect of my life; so I placed less emphasis on their being an extension of me. Consequently, I reacted to their shortcomings with less ego involvement. I saw them more as I was able to see the children of my friends, and I've always been able to give lots of advice to my friends. This detached viewpoint enabled me to act in a more grown-up way. Although I was tired a lot, and my kids could still certainly wear me down, I was able to make decisions about their upbringing without letting my empathy for them get in the way of what I knew to be right."

Many woman are surprised at the versatility of their own children. Once they discover how able their children are to put up with their working, they take renewed pleasure in it.

"I was leaving my three-year-old son five days a week from nine to five. I never would have dreamt of doing that with my first two. I was very nervous about doing it then. When Sam came home tired at the end of each day, I started to think that I was asking too much of him. Had he really fared as well as his nursery school teachers and baby-sitters told me he had? But I hung in there and slowly he adjusted. Furthermore he continued to show signs that he was just as happy and energetic as he had been for three years. As he adjusted to long hours of dealing with environments that weren't his own home, I changed radically. I could see that it was possible, and I lost any ambivalence I originally had. I felt I was a better mother when I was with him than I would have been had I been with him all day."

Most mothers find that the normal demands working mothers must make on children of all ages can be absorbed by children with some profit. Nevertheless, unusual stress—long absences in addition to work-hour absences, poor child care chosen in desperation, perpetual changes in schedules or child-care arrangements— all these things can harmfully affect the child of a working mother just as similar strains could affect the child of a woman who is not employed full time.

When both parents work, it seems they must be careful about what additional demands they make on their children, above and beyond those required because of work. Parents can build up a child's self-confidence through repeated assurances that they can be relied on—both emotionally, in their love and support, and practically in the way they organize family life.

I met another woman who had been a schoolteacher for twenty-five years and had brought up five children, too. We talked about how she felt about her children now that they were grown up and away and whether she felt they had suffered from having such a busy mother.

"No, I think my working was good for them and they agree with me. I was busy but I always made time for them too. After all, the expectations I had for them were not superficial. It was necessary that I work and they knew that. So much of what people teach children or how they teach children is unnecessary and the unnecessariness of it rubs off. Children sense this. If we tell them to be quiet or amuse themselves so that we can amuse ourselves, they know that it isn't necessary. Children know, for instance, that most telephone conversations are unnecessary so they behave obnoxiously when their mothers are on the phone. In our family, everyone knew that mother had to have time in the evening to correct papers, so that time was allowed. Now I think my children have grown up to respect other people's needs more easily than some children I have seen."

Demanding concessions from children and adults that are arbitrary or unnecessary is a thankless task. Children resent it. In contrast, working mothers often find that asking children to give a little as part of a united effort is acceptable. Children understand it and can grow up to value it. In fact, they have to learn it anyway.

Mothers I have interviewed who did not take time off from work to have a family tell me that their children take their parents' working for granted. They're not resentful—they've never known anything else. They take what they get, and what they get is some very good parental care. "In our household," a forty-six-year-old mother of two grown children told me, "it was just like kids grow up and learn that mommy wears glasses or mommy has one leg. In our household, it was mommy and daddy work. And it was just the way our family was. It was no big deal."

The children of women who go back to work have it harder. They go through some initial trauma. But, it seems that if the *parents* are convinced that this is the way things should be, and if they consistently play it out that way, children soon learn to adjust to it, trust it, and take it for granted too. In both cases, parents are assuring the children that this is a *necessary* situation.

Once all conflict has been erased, parents and children can find their own lives and take their family togetherness as an enrichment of what they have on their own. It's not the cold, dry domestic housekeeping relationship that so many of us associate with keeping a home running. It's getting together at the end of a day to see people we truly care about.

A parental fantasy of the future might go something like this: spring 1985—Young mother decides to become housewife and rear children herself—How exhausting, her friends exclaim. Do you think the children will suffer?

five

THE PSYCHOLOGICAL PARENT

Many . . . American fathers have their optic nerves trained to greater visions; their obligations to their children are much less important than their obligations of time and energy to the company, a cause or some vague goal about "getting ahead in the world." These fathers sing all the right notes about loving their children, but it is often love at a distance. In between is a space that the children see all too well, and may want to close. But they can't because their fathers are absent most of the time. COLMAN MCCARTHY, "The State of Fatherland and the Comfort of Continuity," the Washington *Post*, June 17, 1973

Almost all the working mothers I interviewed for this book had one thing in common: they were overworked and tired; many were lonely. Many of them found it difficult to pinpoint the cause of their distress. They had, for the most part, worked out compromises in their family's life-style. Looking around, many could see they had it better than other women, and they wouldn't consider trading positions with the wives who were staying home. They enjoyed their work. In general they felt good about what they were doing with their children. They felt their husbands were "better" than other husbands, more helpful. Some felt their marital relations were more grown up and exciting than those of most of their neighbors and friends with more traditional arrangements. Almost every woman remarked at some point, "I think I have the best of both worlds." They thrived in the variety of their lives.

Less than a handful of women told me that they were waiting for the day when they could quit. Even the most hard-pressed women —with assembly-line or routine corporate jobs—felt their work was fundamental to their sense of independence and contribution. They valued their paychecks both for literal and symbolic reasons. And they were most pleased with their lives when they compared the way they lived with the alternatives.

But I began to sense that the excitement and satisfaction of working mothers also had a darker side—certainly there were problems we weren't confronting; when I asked women to tell me about their fantasies, we got into some areas too sensitive to discuss at first.

Working mothers tended to answer my query of their favorite fantasy with different versions of one basic theme: "I'd like to have time to be alone, and read, or do whatever I want for a while. I have no time that is unscheduled."

Other mothers, women without careers or jobs of some sort, may crave time off alone too, but when I talked with them I didn't hear or sense the same intensity. Some of these women, in fact, told me they fantasized about having a career, a good job, going off to work every morning like their husbands.

But working mothers, every single one I talked to, dreamed and craved time alone, to read, relax, or think. One woman put it this way:

"When I get home from work at suppertime I often resent the fact that I have to work again, at getting supper, helping the kids with the homework, etc. I resent that because, for instance, the photographer I work with goes back to his hotel, has a drink, and unwinds, while I move into second gear. When my husband is home, he helps a lot, but he's a doctor, and often he isn't there when I get home. I'm jealous that the photographer can have his drink, see a movie, or watch television and be rested and fresh the next morning."

She admitted, however, that returning to a solitary hotel room is a lonely, unloving way to end a day. It's not much fun to eat supper in a restaurant alone with the latest edition of the local newspaper propped in front of you. When I asked the husbands of working mothers what their ultimate fantasy was, they said nothing about wanting to be alone. They wanted a variety of things

—more money, more time for their hobbies, or golfing, the wherewithal to travel with their families or wives.

But working mothers wanted to be alone. I felt this was an important clue to a condition common to working mothers that perhaps wasn't fully understood. Why, I wondered, did working mothers yearn to be alone, when their husbands and children didn't?

I interviewed one husband who had taken care of his children for two weeks while his wife was on a business trip. "The older kids were no problem, but the four-year-old! I couldn't relax for a minute," he told me. "I knew I couldn't let up, had to know what he was up to every minute of the day. I didn't have time for anything but child care until he was asleep. I did my reading late at night, sometimes until two or three in the morning. I'd never known anything like it."

His remarks stayed with me for some time. I was mindful that many women told me how concerned they were about their children, even at work. Why could men make a cleaner break between their domestic and professional lives?

So I began to ask men and women which one of them was the "psychological parent" in their household. I defined the "psychological parent" as the person who is always mindful of—who always feels a direct personal responsibility for the whereabouts and the feelings of each child. Who knows what's happening inside the head of each child, all the time? Who knows what emotional supports they need, what size shoes they wear, what diseases they've been exposed to, who their teachers are, what kind of work the first grade does, what new math is all about, who their friends are, who the parents of their friends are, what the current nightmares are, how the baby lies—on his stomach or back—how tightly to bind the blanket in infancy, and so on.

Without exception, the women answered, "I do." And rarely did a husband disagree.

A woman who is a free-lance photographer and writer (her husband is a Wall Street broker) said: "We had discussed endlessly all the problems of bringing up children before we had one. We wanted equal parenting. We took great pains to see that we would both have time to work. As much as we needed. But come the baby, I was the one who felt the baby needed one of us around.

"I was the one who felt bad about leaving him all day. I was the one who cut down on the working hours. In the morning when it was time for both of us to leave, I felt like staying because those little tiny arms in that crib seemed to need one of us, and I guess I thought it was me. I felt terrible because I'd gone into this with the idea that *both* of us should be tuned in. But it was always me who felt guilty about how much baby-sitting we used. My husband apparently could go off to the subway and forget. I never could. I thought about that baby all day. What was happening at this very moment? Was he needing *me*? I found it hard to work. But his work never suffered. *He* never suffered."

Another woman told me, "I often think, 'If I died, you [her husband] would see a whole other world. You would see the black bugs under the carpets.' There is a whole other world order that could impose itself if I crashed into a tree trunk! Then I imagine my husband kneeling at my tombstone, and saying, 'Darling, I had no idea! Please come back from heaven and tell me how to advertise for a new baby-sitter. All I want is just one word about the special way you cram the dryer door shut with the old broken stool, what you say to Susie when she wakes up at 2 A.M., how you confront that sadistic pediatrician, tell me why Max messes his pants only in the sandbox."

Another woman, a free-lance writer, told me, "When we first moved to Cambridge we had a week of unpleasantness. We hadn't moved in completely and we hadn't yet gotten our baby-sitter and Tom was of course teaching for the first time. It was an enormous amount of work for him. In looking back on it I see that I put out more bad vibes than I should have. I said to Tom, 'Could you give me x amount of time, like two or three hours?' Then he pulled out this yellow legal pad and he divided it into fifteen-minute periods. This was really verging on madness. And he said, 'Okay, you do this for fifteen minutes, and I'll do that.' And I said, 'Tom, I'm not looking for fifty-fifty. I'm just asking for a little bit of time that will be solid.' Tom completely misinterpreted what I wanted. I kept saying, 'I'm not after "pseudo equality." I want you to do your courses. I understand what is going on. But I can't get my child into a school and go to the local supermarket without some moments by myself.' So I told him to understand what I was asking for, not to give me more than that."

"Don't try to give me more than I am asking for," many working mothers seem to insist. They stop midway on the road to liberation because they have come so far and because they don't want to be placed on yet another pedestal. Unable to define the source of their unrest, they are reluctant to presume they should be "given" the right to be relieved of the role as the *only* psychological parent.

A father of three who had begun to sense this inequality of parenting talked to me about it. We sat in a living room that hinted at past elegance. The velvet sofa and cream-colored carpet were now scattered with children's things—books half read, a pair of ripped snow pants, a back pack with homework laid out on top of it, a Monopoly game unfinished on the coffee table. The furniture looked worn, as if any restrictions where the children were concerned had been suspended long ago.

"When my wife had our first child, she went to an obstetrician who saw the relationship as strictly between her and him. He never asked to meet me and we never thought to suggest it. I never met him until he announced in a waiting room that I'd had a boy. When Joan had her third baby, we'd changed our feelings about childbirth and attended natural childbirth classes. I was in the delivery room through the entire process. It was an easy, uncomplicated, quite marvelous birth. At thirty-six, I'd had an unforgettable experience. I told my wife the next day, 'Now I think I know what it is for a woman to give birth. I mean, I felt that all the way through.'

"I don't know for sure whether it was that experience or years I'd already spent as a father, but I've felt as responsible for that life as my wife does, and that feeling has made me take an interest and hourly responsibility for my son's life. I would feel insulted or wounded now if my wife felt I wasn't just as capable of taking care of the children as she is."

His wife, however, admitted that in spite of her willing and able husband, she continued to feel that *she* was the psychological parent.

"I still feel something profound, intuitive, that I am the one who will see that their seat belts are buckled, that their lunch box contains just what is expected, that they will have a balanced diet, that when they get home late from school, I'll be the one to find out why."

Women find it difficult to relinquish this role even when they are offered the option. Mothers have taken on the chief parental role partly because they have been sure no one could care that much, partly because they are convinced that their husbands *can't* care that much, and partly because they know their husbands haven't had to worry about the children in the same way mothers have.

Women tend to ask for tangibles. The women's movement has encouraged even the most conventional and satisfied women to ask for help with housework. But women don't know how to ask for a *total* sense of responsibility. We've chuckled so long at the ineptness of men where raising children is concerned that we have come to believe that ineptness is a masculine trait.

Another husband, divorced, had arranged to care for his two children every other month, alternating with his former wife. The first time he handed them over, after a solid month of parental care, he gasped with relief. He was like a hundred other husbands. He had never known.

Many mothers feel the women's movement has demeaned childrearing as a viable alternative, along with certain limiting and poorly paid jobs (secretarial positions, researchers, aids or assistants of any kind). The consequences for working mothers are often painful. Although she is the parent who "knows all" about her own children, she must maintain a different posture in her place of work.

Grace had joined a large law firm as soon as she graduated from law school. She had three children at the time. Now, six years later, she told me that the women's movement and affirmative action plans had made women in business anxious—wanting to prove they're not just there because of a "quota" system.

"I've noticed lately that it is more common for the men here to be caught talking about their children than it is for women. I don't think that's because men are doing more 'mothering' but because we are afraid that if we talk about our children in the lounge, at lunch, or in the halls, we will be labeled 'mothers,' not professionals. We are burning with the sense that we are examples here. We're the lucky representatives of a minority. We have to meet a range of expectations all the time. We would be doing other women a disservice if we were known to be preoccupied with our children while on the job. We keep pretending that it's nothing to work full time and also maintain a family full time."

Priscilla had one child and worked in a literary agency. She had similar problems.

"Last spring my one-year-old daughter had to have a relatively simple eye operation. The operation was on a Thursday and I wanted badly to take three or four days off to be with her that week. I knew, however, that if I told my colleagues, all male, that I was staying home because of my baby, they would say to themselves, 'See, that's what happens when you let women on the staff.' I saw myself as a model for all the young women in the office who were either secretaries or training to be agents. I am the only mother, and I felt I had to show them that women could be mothers and still be professional. So I didn't stay home, and felt conflicted all week. Why should I have to prove anything?"

These women were trying to rid themselves of an image—the presumption that to be a woman means you alone can really know or care about children, that careers have to be pursued with that limitation. Our natural *and conditioned* assumption of infant care starts in the hospital and hits full force at home. It is often the source of "postpartum blues" after a first child. Women gain something in the birth process—a baby. But they lose something, and they are often the only family members who feel a sense of loss even as they experience a full sense of pleasure and pride. They lose a sense of freedom, a private assumption that they are answerable mostly and only to themselves. If a mother falters in her new role as mother, at worst her baby might die. So women take on the responsibility for their babies silently, unquestioningly, without complaint. Slowly that silent responsibility becomes incorporated into their lives.

No matter how much marriages are changed by children, women's private lives change more than men's. This psychological string between mother and child, moreover, is considered a professional drawback. Many male employers voice this assumption when they talk about the problems of hiring mothers. "I know that she'll make all kinds of accommodations to see that there is child care for her children, but if I give her this job, I always have to be mindful that at some time she'll *want* to be at home with the kids."

One feminist mother told me, "When I was interviewing for

my first job out of law school, the recruiters—all men—would invariably ask at the beginning of the interview, 'How many children do you have, Mrs. Minsky?' I would retort, 'And how many children do you have, Mr. Jones?' Can you imagine his asking a male graduate the same question?"

Although women, like men, want careers, children have "counted" more in a woman's life. So far the battle lines, such as they are, have been drawn between women and employers. But the really painful battle, now only reaching minor skirmish proportions, will be between mothers and fathers.

When I started out to interview women for this book, I did not consciously seek women who were feminists. Every once in a while I would come across a woman who had been in a women's consciousness-raising group, or who had participated in some aspects of the movement. But those women were rare. More often, women were aware of the movement only as it had touched on some problem that was pertinent to their lives. Many had read *The Feminine Mystique*, but many years earlier. Few had read any feminist literature since then. The book that professional women seemed to have enjoyed most was Elizabeth Janeway's *Man's World, Woman's Place*.

Few women I talked to were drastically changing their home situations to fit a feminist model. Work had already changed their families.

The stress of being a working mother, I found, was difficult enough without confronting issues that were bound to make matters worse. If the glue holding a marriage together consisted of basic assumptions about a mother's responsibilities, then so be it.

All of this juggling is time-consuming and tiring. No wonder very few successful and professional mothers are also active feminists. Many of the women I interviewed were articulate about women's rights at the office, in the university, at the factory, or in the classroom. But when it came to their families, they had less to say: "My husband is very supportive." "My children have always come first." "He wants me to work if that's what I want to do." "My working hasn't affected his life very much. If anything, he enjoys the extra money we have and thinks I'm more interesting." "He's very proud of me." "The children know I'm still mother first. They're not very impressed with what I do when I'm not here."

The result of this equanimity at home is that for many women the stress of being a working mother is very private. Sometimes they would say nothing about it until we had talked for an hour or two. Slowly they would "remember" times when they had faced problems alone or felt themselves compromising their professional lives for their children. I would often be aware after an interview that I had no real mental picture of the husband. I had listened to lots of stories about children and the responsibilities of childrearing and good professional work, but I hadn't felt the presence of husbands in their talk.

As I listened to my tapes, I realized that only when I was able to assure women that I'd experienced, or at least understood, the nature of these conflicts, was I finally able to get them talking about their misgivings. None of them wanted me to write a book that described the lot of a working mother as hard, lonely, or unrewarding in any way. Because so much of it *was* rewarding.

Many working mothers felt that to relinquish their status as prime psychological parent would mean admitting they couldn't be "a good mother" the way other mothers are. None of these mothers wanted to give up her "mothers ears."

The "mothers ear" concept is rooted in antiquity and sustained by the social and domestic patterns we know so well. New mothers sprout these ears immediately. I got mine the first night home from the hospital with my first child. Christopher was sleeping in a carriage at the foot of our bed. I woke up the instant he first rustled and made those tiny sounds babies do when they are aroused—little muffled snorts. I was wide awake instantly. I lay there frozen, waiting to see, to hear what would happen. As the sounds turned into groggy squeaks, I was out of bed eyes wide open, beads of milk forming at my breasts. A fire alarm couldn't have aroused me more.

Two more children later, at age thirty-five, I still respond as if I had been training all my life to get up in the middle of the night and nurse a baby, cradle it, clean it, and go back to sleep, instantly. I still hear a child cough in the middle of the night. I wake up at the sound of a footstep in the house—provided it's the familiar rustle of feet pajamas padding to the bathroom. I never wake up when the dog, massive as he is, drops his bones to a new position on the hardwood floor. But if my four-year-old son rolls off his bed and onto the floor at 2 A.M., I'm there before the echoes of that modest thud have stopped reverberating. My husband can get up in the wee hours, turn on a light and read, and I'll never know a thing about it, because *I haven't been called to duty*. But if any small body has a nightmare, I'm there before the first wail has subsided.

My husband, on the other hand, sleeps through a good many of these minor calamities—unless he's being awfully cagey. But not all of them. Even when he tells me he'll get up on a particular night so that I can sleep straight through, I still wake up and stay awake until everything's settled. I can't fake it. I have to ask him as he crawls back to bed if "they need me."

A mother's ears operate in the daytime too. If seven kids are out in the backyard and one of them starts to cry, I know instantly if it is mine. I can also tell from the kitchen whether my child is hurt, badly or just a little, whether he is merely outraged, whether he got what he asked for or was surprised by an unjust attack, whether he was on the way in to get me, or lying there rolled up with pain and indignation, whether a sister or brother hit him, or perhaps a friend. I know when I answer the phone if the voice on the other end is going to give me news of a child in trouble. Two years ago my dearest friend had a son who was killed in an automobile accident. She told me that when her friends came to find her to tell her, she was working outside in the yard. She turned to see them and knew instantly what had happened.

This maternal tuning-in seems never to leave women who go off to work. They sit at their desks in offices, prone, stiff with anticipation. I don't think this will, nor am I proposing that it ever should, stop. Children need this sort of parental sensitivity. They can sense when someone is absolutely committed to listening for and to them. As they get older, and reach their teens, this listening is still important. It means that when something is festering inside a child, when he or she is confused, worried, anxious, an adult who loves is really there to help, to sense without being told, to respond without being asked. More fathers, however, need to be equipped with these ears.

It's not that most fathers don't try to become a part of their children's lives. But once trained to hand over an important aspect of childrearing to their wives, they can have difficulty tuning in on matters involving sheer feeling. You can hear this in a telephone conversation between a father and mother and their college-aged child. The father asks how *things are* there. "Got some good courses? How's the money holding out? Let us know if you need anything. Be sure to write to your mother." Then the mother adds, "Hi, dear, how *are* you?" It's a cue to discuss anything that's personal, intimate, needful, worrisome, special. Most mothers have been handed, and have accepted, this role of confidante and mediator.

In my interviews I found a tremendous imbalance in the parental concerns of working mothers and fathers. I didn't expect to find all responsibilities parceled out on a fifty-fifty basis, nor did I find that women wanted it that way. Just about everybody pooh-poohed marriage contracts, and tended to think of fifty-fifty negotiating as the last resort in an already bad marriage. "If you care about each other, you want to help each other in whatever way is needed. I help him with some things, he helps me with some things. We don't need to talk about it all the time. It's natural. It grows out of our feelings for each other." But the women who said that found it difficult to articulate their need for *parental initiative*. Most women willing to admit they wanted more of that initiative from their husbands were new mothers, still shocked by their sense of total responsibility for another life.

One woman who had her first child in the midst of a blooming career in publishing, and took off only four weeks to recover from childbirth—two of those weeks working at home—described her first few months back on the job. "The big change for me was this tremendous sense of being needed all the time. I was needed at the office and I loved that feeling. I knew I had made myself needed there. But now I was needed at home too. I don't mean I was needed there *all* the time. But I was acutely aware of how indispensable I was. No one could do either job the way I could. No one could do it as well. No one knew all that I did. It was overwhelming. I found myself walking around deeply engrossed in thinking about it. It was as if I had replaced my own mother. Now it was my turn. I had grown up."

Many men, on the other hand, often feel superfluous during the same period. When they get home, their wives are busy with the business of taking care of a new baby. Dr. Spock is not very helpful on this point. Says Spock:

> Some fathers have been brought up to think that the care of babies and children is the mother's job entirely. But a man can be a warm father and a real man at the same time. We know that the father's closeness and friendliness to his chil-

dren will have a vital effect on their spirits and characters for the rest of their lives. So the time for him to begin being a real father is right at the start. It's easiest then. The father and mother can learn together. . . . Of course, I don't mean that the father has to give just as many bottles or change just as many diapers as the mother. But it's fine for him to do these things occasionally. He might make the formula on Sunday.

Spock concludes: "Of course, there are some fathers who get gooseflesh at the very idea of helping to take care of a baby, and there's no good to be gained by trying to force them. Most of them come around to enjoying their children later 'when they're more like real people.'"*

Dr. Spock, a well-meaning and profoundly sensitive man, must have been aware of the likely impact of his words and so offered advice ambiguous enough so that he couldn't be blamed for upsetting a million marriages. But he was setting out to comfort a generation of mothers brought up on a set of premises that now seem archaic. For the 51 per cent of American working women with children under five, his advice will seem pretty hollow.

If both parents are going to approach equality as psychological parents, fathers have to get over their squeamishness. Recall the advice of Mary, who told her husband that if he weren't willing to care for and know his children when they were little, he couldn't expect to step in later on. It doesn't seem enough to try to catch up when the children are more like "real people" because they will already have established a pattern of intimacy with one parent, and, more important, the mother will have simply assumed the lion's share of this kind of parenting.

The women I spoke with did not leave me with the feeling that their solitary burdens were all Dr. Spock's fault, or all their husbands' fault. Ingrid, for example, clearly felt her role as primary household manager and primary childrearer was due as much to her own conscious choice as to any pressure from her husband. "My blocking was as much internal as external," she said.

Many women, however, admit that they had "gooseflesh" when confronted with a new baby. Taking care of an infant does not always seem so natural to women either. I talked with one woman, a college administrator, in her office, a plush, but businesslike room, barren of any of the familiar signs of children. No

* Baby and Child Care, pp. 30–31.

photos, nursery school drawings, clay ashtrays, or other memora-
bilia. She had stayed home one month with her first child, then
fled back to her office.

"During the month that I stayed home, I felt so unoccupied. I
don't know what to do with unstructured time, I wasn't doing *anything*. We had a fairly small apartment and hired a cleaning lady.
So I didn't have anything to do except take care of a little baby,
and you can only do so much of that. It was nice to be able to
read and pursue my own interests, but, I thought, I don't want to
do *just* that. I have to do something. I'm not accomplishing anything. The whole period was hard because I was so unused to
babies. I remember bringing Susie home and my husband started
to cry and I started to cry. I gather that's a very common thing,
but I didn't feel intuitively that this was what I was supposed to
do. I wasn't a very natural mother."

As Susie got older and a second daughter came along, this
mother *learned* to be a parent. Even so, she needs lots of reinforcement and admits that she has lots to be concerned about
now.

"Because of my inexperience I always wonder whether I'm
doing the right thing. When we get into bad phases and the kids
seem unhappy or upset, I think, 'Is it because I'm working?'
Where discipline is concerned, I wonder if my children are confused and so have more discipline problems because a number of
people take care of them, and have different expectations of them.
But the nursery school teachers tell me Susie has no problems, so
I get reinforcement."

How much of a psychological parent was this woman's husband?

"My husband is very good in a pinch and on holidays he helps
around. He never minds caring for the children but he never gears
his schedule to child care, and household duties, no. He will do
any of those things if he has time. He's co-operative but it's a very
traditional relationship. In the very beginning he didn't think he
wanted his wife to work. He certainly didn't think I should work
after we had children. His attitude now is, as long as I can handle
it, the house and everything, it's fine."

Some women suffer more than others over this problem.
Women who have had a rough time getting back to work, have
gone through some major conflict, or stepped way out of a mold—

they tend to carry the problems of their children with them all the time.

Alice lived in a small town in Indiana. She was a conservative, low-key woman who had stayed home with two children for seven years. Her husband worked for a huge steel company. His salary had reached $20,000 a year and they had paid off all but $5,000 of their mortgage on a small ranch-style house when she decided to go back to work—in a bank. She'd worked as a teller before marriage and several of her friends—not married—were working in their local savings bank. As soon as she mentioned her plans to her family, her mother, who lived in Kansas, came for a visit "to see what was wrong." Her next-door neighbor tried to persuade her that she was still needed by her children—her neighbor had six children and both she and her husband felt strongly that a woman's place was in the home. Alice waited another year before "sneaking" down to the bank to have an interview with the personnel director. When I met her she had been working four years and still worried about whether she was right or wrong.

"My biggest problem is that I agonize a lot and I have no rules to go by. My husband is supportive of my working but he could never understand the dilemmas I'm faced with. He often tells me I'm just being silly and there's nothing to worry about. I think he's trying to tell me that it's all right if I work, but then he doesn't know what maternal guilt is all about."

Women with jobs that offer less prestige or salary than their husband's tend to seem reluctant to assign as much value to their time. Though they may feel that housework and mothering are demeaning, it never seems to occur to them to ask their husbands to help out.

Women whose husbands have jobs that provide little self-esteem seem to make few domestic demands on them in order to help them maintain a traditional manly image. Then, if their own jobs are equally unvalued, they cling to their childrearing concerns as a source of worthiness.

Gladys worked as a cashier at a supermarket. Her husband was a shipper for stationary goods. They lived in a triple-decker house in a working-class suburb of Boston, with their six children. They had the same hours, although he made slightly more money than she did. But their work was physical, she on her feet all day and he driving a truck. She had never asked him for any child-care or

daily domestic help. In their living room sat an over-stuffed loung-
ing chair, religiously reserved for his use at the end of each day.
Gladys, on the other hand, took considerable pride in her clean,
neatly dressed children, her scrubbed apartment, and her husband's "man of the family" pose.

"Each morning all eight of us get up at 6:30 and prepare to go
someplace. The kids go to school, my husband goes on the road,
and I go to the store. But here's the difference: while he is off totally absorbed in trucking paper supplies, I am standing right opposite a big clock on the wall. I watch that clock all day, ticking
off the things that my kids are doing. I think, it's twelve o'clock,
Tommy is going to Louise's house for lunch, Sally is supposed to
see that Steve gets to the baby-sitter's. It's two o'clock, three of
them are getting home, I have to call in to see that everything is
all right. I have them on my mind all the time. They're always
with me."

Being the primary psychological parent means that most
women never leave for work with a clear sense of division between
home and office. It isn't that women don't perform well at their
jobs. They do. Barbara Walters once said that the key to her success was that she worked harder than anyone else. She doesn't
need to convince me. Ambitious working mothers work very hard
to be superb in two places, home and office. They are damned if
anyone is going to point a finger at them and say they are bad
mothers or inadequate in any way. Ambitious fathers work very
hard at their jobs and they prove that they aren't inadequate. If
the kids are in trouble, that's because the mother is working. Even
though many parents quarrel about that assumption, in a crunch
they accept its conventional wisdom.

"My children have always come first. If I ever felt that my
working was doing them harm, I would quit. There's no question
about that. I know that and my husband knows that. We agree
on it. I'm a mother first."

At some future date those words might change in response to
the changing times. If asked, parents might rephrase that declara-
tion: "Our children come first in our lives. If we ever feel that our
work is harming them, we will both cut back on our work loads.
We both agree on that." A liberated fantasy? Or a coming necessity?

six

A MOTHER'S LEGACY:
AN ANCESTRAL FORMULA
FOR WORKING PARENTS

*I'm a feminist and the mother of three daughters. I work full time
fifty weeks out of a year and I say to myself once in a while, "What
will my girls think of that?" Do you think they'll grow up wishing I
was more to them? Could I have spent better time with them? How
can I give them a legacy of independence when I count on baby-sitters and teachers to do much of the traditional maternal teaching?
It's a source of great concern to me, and I wonder if I can count on
my words of wisdom to carry them through life. Maybe what someone else says to them will mean more to them.* A THIRTY-FOUR-
YEAR-OLD ELECTRICAL ENGINEER

Men and women get a lot from their mothers, much of it life-sus-
taining and worthy of respect and affection. They also accumulate
"signals" from both parents, evidence that shapes their own developing views—toward marriage, parenthood, family dynamics, and
toward the complex issues that characterize the experiences of
working mothers.

"When we were first married," said Nan, a young mother, "I
found it difficult to accept my husband's offer of help around the
house. I grew up in a family where my father wouldn't lift a
finger, and Bob grew up in a family where his father and mother
both worked. His father regularly did the washing and other
household chores, and even before we had children Bob would do
the vacuuming and things like that. I found it humiliating. I ac-

cepted it but I felt guilty. Occasionally I'll forget to do the laundry and he'll do it over the weekend. I'm always filled with embarrassment.

"My mother *didn't* work, so my maternal model was a different sort altogether. She led a very restricted life and I found it hard to figure out a way to have more freedom, more options, more mobility than my mother had known."

Nan didn't start out as a very strongly motivated working mother. Although her husband was willing and trained to do his share of the housework, she found his eagerness puzzling. When she graduated from college, the same year as her husband, she was confused. Where, she said, do I go from here?

"Part of my fantasy is that if I had been a boy I'd have felt pressure to decide on a profession instead of stopping after college. Working against that pressure, in me, was a lot of personal confusion. I took time to sort things out for myself. I know a lot of young men who are doing that these days too. I had babies, however, and it wasn't until after they were born that I thought about a profession."

Nan is in her early thirties. She has two children, a five-bedroom house in the suburbs, and a live-in baby-sitter. Nan considers herself a part-time worker, but her hours add up to full-time employment. She teaches two classes at an adult education center—one in ceramics, one in dance—and is writing a book. Occasionally she picks up magazine work and she and her husband have collaborated on a number of book reviews.

She does not, however, see herself as very productive. "I have a lot of bad feelings about not being able to earn as much money as Bob or to have an outlet for my talent that is constant and secure. He has found his profession but I don't have a career I can call my own."

Nan had grown up as a "Jewish princess." Her mother had seen to it that her wardrobe and her toilette were impeccable every day. Her thick wavy black hair was brushed to a shine—she was a beautiful child, and her skin and color still stand as examples of what fine care can do. She had known she would grow up to be a beautiful woman from the time she was in kindergarten. "I was adored, cherished. I can remember thinking that every time I smiled I made somebody happy." Nan's mother devoted much of her time to the care of her daughter. The rest of her time she devoted to the care of her husband and son.

"I felt that everyone expected me to do something extraordinary with my life and nothing I could do would ever live up to those expectations. I just gave up while I was in college.

"A lot of girls—especially those like myself who came from public school systems where they were really big wheels—came to college with scholarships and inflated ideas about their potential. In a place like Radcliffe, where we were no longer clearly better than everyone else, we began to have grave doubts about ourselves and a lot of us were paralyzed with insecurity and misgivings about our true ability. I felt I couldn't deal with my anxieties about failing and being made a fool of. So I stopped going to a lot of sections."

Marriages, plainly, owe a great deal to our own efforts and dreams, but they are also shaped by our parents' expectations and examples. For Nan, and a great many other working parents I talked to, the lessons of their childhoods immensely complicated the problems of adjustment and self-discovery.

Frannie considered herself a "dabbler" without any real profession. She lived in California with her children and several other young people who rented rooms in her house. When I met her she was divorced. Her children were four and seven and the last several years had been extremely difficult for her. She was a very sensual woman who talked reflectively, as if her words had been carefully chosen. She looked Californian, brown and blond, and she wore gaily colored hand-woven and -embroidered skirts and blouses. She smiled a lot when she talked, which made me think she was determined to make the best of things—at least from now on.

Frannie had worked during her first pregnancy but her experience was all too familiar to women who complain of sexual discrimination:

"I was earning $85 a week as an editorial assistant at a national magazine, with nowhere to go but sidewise. I think I would have turned into a worm if I hadn't worked because I didn't feel very good being pregnant. I was sick a lot and it was good to have a reason to get up in the morning.

"My husband was eager to have a child too, but for theoretical reasons. In retrospect, I see it as a sort of confirmation of his manhood. He didn't really know what it was going to be like. Of course I didn't either.

"I thought, I really want this baby and I really want to be a mother. I planned to stop working and not to start again until I felt ready."

I asked Frannie how seriously she had taken her prospects as a professional woman before and after her marriage. She admitted that the idea of supporting herself with a profession had never occurred to her.

"My lack of concern came from my mother. She's worked and done a lot of things but she disguised the fact that she was doing them. Her family always came first. She was a college sophomore dropout when she got married, but between the time she got married and my graduation from high school, she earned a B.A., M.S., and a Ph.D. from Harvard.

"She made sure her classes were scheduled when the five of us kids were in school so she was always home when we were. Now she thinks that was a mistake. She feels maybe if she had encouraged us to believe it was okay as girls and women to have something as our own, it would have been easier for us.

"She encouraged us to get good marks, but she never made us feel that her career was very important. The family was everything; the family and my father. Whatever he said went. She was totally submissive. He has a lot of intellectual notions about women's liberation now—that it's a good thing, and all that, but he doesn't *live* it. He's not very supportive of my mother. He wants to be, but at heart he expects her to nurture *him*. I'm not sure he knows *how* to give it back to her."

Frannie had been out of college for twelve years when I met her. The first five were chaotic, one odd job after another, followed by an impulsive marriage that ended in a sad divorce. She'd virtually stumbled into motherhood, unaware how drastically a baby would change her life. All this time she was trying to be the woman she thought her mother wanted her to be, trying to be different but without knowing who *she* really was. Her husband eventually had a nervous breakdown, "slowly going mad in front of me," she said. She had her second baby while nursing her husband through his final tailspin. With an infant, another little boy, and a sadness she could barely talk about, Frannie *had* to wake up to the cruel fact that she alone was going to bring up her sons, to provide for them, and, most importantly, *be* with them daily.

Once again Frannie found it difficult to separate her sense of self from her image of mother's daughter. She decided to teach retarded children, and with the help of a day-care center and the financial support of her father, she earned her master's degree and began to work to support her boys.

"But I found out I had just placed myself back into one more nurturing role. I'd be caring for helpless children all day and then come home to care for my own babies. I kept remembering my mother, who seemed to have been everybody's nursemaid and I felt a failure in comparison to her. It was the same way with my marriage. . . . When I first fell in love with Danny, I knew he was a little crazy, mixed up, and also a genius. I thought, well, I will save him and make him better, make him feel wonderful. But it got to be too much for me.

"I have a hard time asking for help and letting people know that I need it. Especially my mother. She is so eager to mother me. It's as though once you put your foot in the door, you'll never get it out again. I'm afraid that once I let her know, I'll be smothered by her. When I need mothering, she is so happy to have the opportunity, she makes me feel like I'm being suffocated."

Frannie's floundering, of course, is not simply a consequence of her mother's willingness to be the perpetual nurturer. But virtually *all* the women I talked with who'd had trouble sorting out the conflicting ambitions in their lives found parallels between their confusion and the mixed signals they felt they'd gotten as children from their mothers.

Natalie is thirty-three years old, she is a tenured professor at one of Massachusetts' most prestigious colleges, and the mother of two children aged three and six. Her story contrasts strikingly with the troubled experiences of Nan and Frannie.

"I was brought up by a mother who never worked, was totally absorbed in her children, and complained bitterly about it. My sister is a lawyer, and she and I were told at a very early age that we'd better find something we could do and *do it*. When my sister and I had children, my mother was horrified, in spite of herself, that we continued working too. But my mother's bitterness—and our talks about it—was one of the important things in my childhood.

"So the prospect of not working is very alarming to me. My husband's mother worked, and I suspect that part of his tolerance of my working comes from the fact that he was brought up that way himself. I think he always wanted a wife who had her own independent thing.

"We got married when we were very young. I was twenty-one and he was twenty-two. We weren't planning babies at that point, but we expected children 'when we grew up.' So we finished graduate school. I felt I *had* to get my degree before I had children, or I'd never finish. I'd seen that happen all around, people trying to write theses and take care of babies. The babies always won.

"I remember one very upsetting visit to a gynecologist who asked me when I was intending to have children. I said, 'Well, not now.' He said, 'Do you think you can just pick and choose everything? It can take you five years to get pregnant.' I never went back to him."

I asked every woman I interviewed whom she had patterned herself after. The three women above are representative of the typical responses. Highly motivated working mothers seemed to produce daughters with strong career motivations. Or else, as with Natalie's mother, frustrated women encouraged their daughters to seek careers—producing similar results. I met women who had mothers without careers of their own but who had been determined to bring up their daughters to have ambitious goals. "Don't fall into my trap" was the message these women picked up from their nonworking mothers.

The maternal legacy is delicate, not easily disguised. Nan's mother, for example, groomed and admired her daughter, all the while suggesting that she would conquer the world. "Do well in school. Always arrange yourself prettily. If you do, the world will be at your feet." Many women who heard that message decided to make someone a terrific wife and mother. But others who'd gone off to win scholarships and degrees at esteemed colleges were confused. They thought themselves too smart to grasp at the first appealing husband-prospect to come along. But if they chose the road to ambition, they risked traveling it alone.

Mothers who had stayed home and hadn't complained delivered another confusing message to their daughters, particularly when they had been treated shabbily by their husbands. These women often became *reverse* models for their daughters.

"I always admired my father most," a Midwestern, thirty-five-year-old mother of three told me. "He had all the fun in life. I didn't have any brothers, and only one older sister, so my father thought of me as the son he didn't have. He treated me better than any other member of the family. I was clearly the favorite child.

"My mother, by contrast, was really our maid. The only real satisfaction she ever got out of life, I think, was her work in our church. She was active and appreciated there, often elected to some office. I suppose that might have been something to admire and model myself after, but by the time I was in high school and college, I had totally rejected the church and saw even that part of her life as rather pathetic.

"My father, on the other hand, was a prosperous contractor who often brought home men *and women* with a whole different handle on life than my mother. They were powerful and self-assured. One woman I admired particularly. She was my father's age and very beautiful. She had a lovely sense of style and I was old enough to see that most of the wives of the men she worked with hated her guts. They smiled and treated her obsequiously, but I knew they feared her. Their husbands, of course, fell all over themselves to charm her. She was a very smart woman—with tremendous self-confidence and élan.

"If I modeled myself after anyone, it was she. But my strongest drive, probably, was to disassociate myself from my mother. Which, I should emphasize, has never been easy. In the years right after my marriage I tried to be a good housewife just to get approval. I finally realized that was a dead end. I was pouring myself a cocktail at 4:30 in the afternoon just to keep from feeling my frustration, my growing hatred of myself. I felt two people were inside of me and I didn't know which one was the stronger.

"Finally the anti-mother won out. I am very ambitious now. The women's movement has helped to bring this all together for me. But even now I struggle with my aggressive ambitious self—I worry that I'm not, somehow, sufficiently feminine."

Women whose mothers had worked through their childhoods seemed to have relatively little difficulty finding their identities both before and after their marriages. Like Natalie, they went

from high school to college to graduate school or a job without
considering once that they would stop. If they did take time off, it
was for pleasure, not to resolve some nettlesome conflict between
ambition and domesticity.

"Whether or not I worked has just never been an issue with
me," a thirty-six-year-old Texas physician explained. "My mother
was a schoolteacher and my father a rancher. Both of my parents
gave me a lot of their time, but they also made it perfectly clear
that people pulled their weight in this world. It would have been
inconceivable for me to graduate from college and get married
right away without career plans. I'm a product of the middle-class
ethic that says you ought to get ahead in life, you ought to be able
to do better than your parents. Neither of my parents had been to
graduate school. So of course they were pleased and probably
relieved that I chose to go into medicine.

"My mother and I used to ride horses a lot together. We would
get home from school at the same time and she would say to me,
'Let's go out for a ride. It's always good for your body if you get
some exercise after you've been using your head for a while.' And
sometimes she would tell me, 'Never go directly from work to
housework. Always go get some fresh air first. After a ride on a
good horse, a woman can always get a second wind.'

"Those were lovely years. When my mother was sixty, and I'd
come home from med school, she would have the horses all
saddled up and tell me to 'get out there and ride some of these
books out of your lungs.' She was as good on a horse then as I
was."

Women who found themselves early, had directed themselves
professionally, usually married more cautiously and somehow selected husbands who could accommodate their way of life. Their
husbands expected them to have independent lives. Most important, their husbands assumed they would have to pull their weight
in managing a household and rearing children.

Four years ago I met once a week with seven other women
who'd formed a consciousness-raising group. We'd been floundering for months with vague and trivial topics. No one seemed to
have a clear idea of what we were trying to accomplish. We were
being very delicate with each other. If one of us said anything
controversial, we tried to clear the air immediately. One night
someone came to the meeting and started talking about her
mother. One by one, we all talked about our mothers, how we felt

about them, what sort of relationship we had with them now, what kind of people they were. Very few of us, we discovered, admired our mothers. The evening went on way beyond the usual cut-off period. When we finally quit, we agreed that we'd reached some important turning point in the direction of our group.

Months later we recalled that meeting and asked ourselves what mothering ought to mean to us now. We were all mothers. Most of us had daughters. Would being feminists help them to see us years later as more supportive? What could we do for our daughters anyhow? Would they have to have consciousness-raising groups too?

None of us knew the answers. Everything we suggested seemed a form of preaching. We would buy books for our children that seemed nonsexist. We would make sure that they had doctors' costumes to play with instead of nurses'. We would sign them up for instructions in physical sports. We would preach the word around the house. All of these things were sure to be helpful, but by themselves they'd probably fall short of the mark.

One of the most important impressions daughters get from their mothers is the way the mother's life is shaped by work. From one's mother a child can realize that a professional career is a realistic possibility, that it's a self-defeating assumption to assume that careerism is either antifeminine or antithetical to domesticity or parenthood. A mother can also see to it, as well as she can, that these assertions aren't undermined by signals of a different sort.

Women who complain over breakfast and dinner that they hate their jobs, are being done in by men at the office, or can't manage the house and still work full time are giving their daughters (and sons) some powerful hints about life's painful "realities."

If being a working mother is hard for some women, it is important to let a daughter know *why*. Even if the answer is extremely painful and embarrassing, working mothers owe it to their daughters to be candid. An observant adolescent daughter who sees her mother working full time and getting no help at home from her husband will likely put two and two together, and possibly come up with the wrong answer.

Many women in just that situation have accepted the two treadmills as a compromise. One Vermont woman told me why she had chosen not to challenge a husband who never lifted a finger in their house. "My husband is not a very sophisticated man. He was brought up by a woman who worshiped his dad and spent her life catering to him. Steve would expect it of me. Now I know it's unreasonable of him. But I decided long ago that I couldn't change him; I could only hurt him. Neither one of us has a lot of education and I guess I've had more experiences in life than he. But he's a good man and has always been gentle with me. I have a lot to be thankful for."

This woman did not see her husband as an unfeeling brute. But her daughters might. They might, furthermore, see her as a submissive, blind, overworked fool—not at all her own view of herself.

I asked this fifty-two-year-old woman if she had ever talked to her two daughters about her life. "Yes, I've had long talks with them. One of them is married, with a baby and a job. She's having a hard time, but not the way I did. With her its inflation and child care."

"I told both Beth and Sara that my work had always been a source of pleasure. We don't need the money now but I still want to work. I'm only a secretary, but I've worked in the same office for twenty-five years and I practically run the place. It gives me a lot of satisfaction. I told them to get that too. And I told them their dad was an old-fashioned guy—which believe me they know because there have been lots of arguments in that direction—but that we love each other. I told them they would find the kind of guy they would love, as I found mine. I work around his faults. And you know? They respect him in a lot of things. He's very quiet, but he's a moral, honest man. They know he's worked hard all his life and they have never seen him be rude to me. He may sit in his Archie Bunker chair and read the paper, but he doesn't yell at me. They see that."

If the maternal legacy is palpable where daughters are concerned, it seems just as crucial for sons. The interviews for this book suggest that the best husband for a working wife seems to be one who has been raised by a helpful father *and* a working mother. The men I met who had working mothers expected their wives to be independent and busy. They expected, for the most part, to take on a considerable share of the domestic turmoil and responsibilities.

The relationship between mother and son, of course, is a highly charged one. Freud and Oedipus aside, men seem to like their wives to regard them with *at least* the same respect and care that their mothers showed for their fathers. It seems a cruel blow to many men that after twenty-odd years of watching their fathers get first-class treatment from the first woman they ever loved, they can't get the same nurturing and attention. The husbands of working mothers are even more on edge over this issue as they strive to compete with their own babies and a boss or job over which they have no control.

Many men who marry liberated, competent, working women agree to have a child and to take on an equal burden of raising that child. But the likelihood is these men will have few friends who will share their views. The chances are great that they observed no such pattern in their own childhoods.

I have a friend, a doctor, who says he was brought up by a "good Jewish mother." He married, at thirty, a woman with a Ph.D. in government, and they worked for five years before having their first child. His wife stayed home for six months, then went back to the college campus. The two of them are currently battling for their lives. "We're taking turns with *everything*," he told me grimly. "I can't even go to the bathroom unless it fits into the schedule. That's not the way *I* was brought up."

Working mothers have a responsibility toward their sons, of course, and a wife who plays doormat to her husband's patriarchal vanity is teaching her sons a lesson that could—unless they're lucky enough to find a wife modeled after Mother—land them in the divorce courts. I interviewed a man who was married to a buyer in a department store. Her hours were regular, but the pressure during certain seasons was considerable. Moreover, she often had to travel to New York on buying trips. They had one child, a six-year-old girl. I met him at his apartment on an evening when his wife was away. She had been gone for two nights, and would be back in two more. Although he talked about the problems of being a "working mother," he seemed competent enough to me. Their apartment was "decorated" and neat. Life seemed to be very well organized. But, he explained, domestic harmony had come with difficulty.

"My mother was a pediatrician with four children. All of us have grown up to marry women with careers. But interestingly enough, three of us have discovered that we were not model husbands. Our father was a lawyer, a very successful one, and he made much more money than my mother. She arranged her office hours around our school hours and when dad came home, everything was taken care of. The fact that we never saw him doing housework, or taking care of our needs in any way, we all feel was important to our expectations.

"We never saw him abuse my mother. In fact, he was very proud of her. Often he would tell us to find a wife like his. He held her up on an intellectual pedestal for us to admire. But he never altered his own traditional husband's role to accommodate her in any way. It never occurred to any of us that our wives wouldn't do the same. The first time my wife sent me to the laundromat, I was aghast. I only went because I was so astonished I didn't know what else to do."

A poll conducted by the Roper Organization, and paid for by the Virginia Slims cigarette people, concluded that women in 1974 were opting for "egalitarian marriage." Almost half (46 per cent) of them say they prefer a marriage "where husband and wife share responsibilities more—both work, both share homemaking and child responsibilities." Furthermore, more than half (52 per cent) say they want to combine a career with marriage and raising children. In 1970 only 40 per cent of those women polled in a similar survey supported efforts to change or strengthen their status. In 1974, 57 per cent wanted those changes and only 25 per cent opposed them. If that trend continues, by the time my four-year-old son is ready to marry, he'll have a hard time finding a wife who won't tell him to pick up his own socks, a chore he's already found intolerable.

CHILD CARE

Their most sensitive problem, working parents agree, is the matter of child care. Among the people I talked with, however, only rarely were both parents involved in deciding how to solve the problem. For the most part, fathers seem to be brought into the process only when wives are unable to make a decision independently. Even then, the logistics and communication tend to be left to mothers. The search for someone to care for the children seems so exclusively a mother's job that some people I talked with wondered if the pattern was not due to sheer possessiveness.

Working mothers seem to have two basic beliefs which support their assumption of this responsibility. First, the assumption that it's their duty simply because they're mothers; if they want to work and be mothers at the same time, they have to find a way to manage the problem of children. This is as true for mothers of newborn infants as it is for older women with school-aged children; as true for women with high-paying jobs as for women merely bringing in "pin money"; as true for veterans of the women's movement as for women who have fiercely ignored it.

Second, most women feel their work is less important than their husbands'. When it comes to making arrangements for the house or children, they feel paralyzed at the thought of suggesting that their husbands give up valuable time or energy in order to help arrange for child care.

One woman I talked to, a brilliant social scientist with two small boys, aged three and five, was married to a struggling architect. She made "a little more" than he. "But," said she, "he is much more talented than I am and he earns less, in part, because of our decision to live here in the East where his field is so crowded." She took care of all the hiring of household help and the organization of the household. Her office was in their home, so that she could be around the boys during the day. "You might say I'm still the primary household manager," she said.

I interviewed another couple, both doctors. She had taken a year out of her training for each of two children, and then, once in practice, worked only while her children were in school. "I've always made the arrangements for the children except when I was a resident and had to use my husband for the nights I was on duty. Even then I tried to arrange my schedule to fit his off-duty nights."

Although she had wanted to go into surgery, she changed her specialty when she learned she was pregnant. She chose dermatology because she knew child care would thus be easier to arrange. Even so, she was earning almost twice her husband's salary, five years past her residency. She insists, however, that her husband is "a more brilliant physician" than she can ever be.

Many of the working women I talked to tended to see their husbands' careers as sacrosanct. No matter how viable, in the practical sense, an alternative arrangement might be, they rarely violate this most basic traditional assumption. So child care becomes the woman's problem, and if she can't solve it, she can't work.

This means that women have to learn how to interview for child care, advertise for it, try it out, work with it, and, once their children reach nursery school age, perform scouting and selection missions. As one woman put it, "I have two children. We wanted four. But I can't go through *all that* again. It's not the baby business I can't go through—I love babies. It's the search for the good 'nanny' I can't face."

Here are some of the child-care solutions the people I talked with had tried.

DAY CARE

Day care is one solution, yet many women say they want no part of it. The decision to stay away from day care does not seem to be a function of class. Rich or poor, educated or not, many women object to the very idea of day care—that is, to having their children cared for in an "institution." So far, only academic mothers, as a group, seem to have warmed to the idea. They are, however, the women with greatest access to good day care—they can afford it and campuses have made it available, at least for the lucky few.

But women who find good day care available and learn to enjoy it constitute a tiny minority. According to the U. S. Department of Labor, almost half of the preschool children of working mothers are cared for in their homes; not quite a third are cared for in someone else's home; roughly 5 per cent are placed in group-care centers; the rest have other arrangements. Some are cared for by their mother while she works; others are "latch-key children" who care for themselves.

It's not only that day care is rarely available—or that it doesn't work. Most women simply don't know what good day care is, don't know how to start and organize a center where facilities aren't already in operation, and are likely to be overwhelmed by the obstacles that arise once a center gets going.

Hostility toward day care seems to come from a variety of apprehensions, not all of them convincingly rational. Most women I talked with said they had never seen a day-care center. "To tell the truth, I've never even been in one," many women told me. "I wouldn't know what to expect." Some echoed Dr. Spock, "I think day care is fine if that is all you have available. But I wouldn't use it unless I had to." Unaware that most day care (unless government or industry funded) costs about the same as at-home help, women who can afford a private housekeeper/ nurse persist in their view of day care as a necessary evil for women who *have* to use it. The cost of full-time day care ranges from $25 to $65 a week, including transportation. Many women pay that much for a live-in helper, or *au pair* girl. Although au pair girls also get board and room, families with these arrangements often get evening and weekend child care as well, which in most urban communities means the situations offer roughly the same value.

The most common explanation offered by women who don't want to use day care is the feeling that preschool children and infants are "better off" if they can be kept at home during the day. Although many women are articulate on this point, others "just feel that way." The Feldmans from Ithaca, New York, reported that many lower-class women have a negative attitude toward day care because it seems like school. "They want their kids to have fun; there's plenty of time for them to go to school later." Day-care centers are thought of as schools by *both* middle- and lower-class parents, especially for two- to five-year-old children. They are seen as institutions that can hardly give the kind of warm loving care mothers want for their small children.

Class attitudes toward day care seem particularly ironic. While middle-class mothers believe centers are primarily for lower-class families, lower-class mothers see them as middle-class establishments far beyond their financial reach.

Day care's bad reputation is not, of course, always undeserved. A "bad" day-care center is a very sad place indeed, for reasons to be discussed shortly. But even "good" centers seem to have logistical problems built into the system that trouble some among even the most willing parents. The most common problem is a sick child. A mother with help at home can go to work when a child has chicken pox. But if she's counting on day care, and must leave her child at home, she has to hire someone to back her up, leaving many with the feeling that day care is more trouble than it's worth.

Another common complaint from women with several children, some old enough to go to school, is that too many separate arrangements are needed—that they might as well put the package together and find a single solution that will fit all the children's schedules—a housekeeper who is *always* there.

Many communities have day-care centers open only from 8 or 9 A.M. to 5 P.M. For a commuting parent, these hours may not be sufficient. Where the hours are sufficiently elastic, women without a car face still another logistical problem. Getting back and forth can mean extra hours away from the child, and a great deal of additional expense. A woman in California, who spends hours on public transportation getting from home to day-care center to her job and then back again: "It takes me two hours to complete the cycle each way. Lugging my briefcase and his gear, I'm so tired when we get home for supper I have to push hard to give him the kind of attention a three-year-old needs."

For most women, however, fear of social stigma, rather than logistics, seems to be what keeps them from using or recommending day care. "People in this neighborhood think ill enough of me for working in the first place. Imagine what they'd think if I put my children in a center! At least I have a kind, grandmotherly housekeeper who keeps their noses clean and settles them into their own beds."

Even so, a great many women find day-care centers a virtual necessity. Those who have seen well-run day-care centers, the sort that offer much more than custodial care, declare them a greatly preferred alternative to the hassle involved in finding and paying for housekeepers, nannys, or other mother substitutes in the home.

Because it is expensive, in some measure a parent substitute, and thus seemingly a threat to traditional childrearing patterns, as well as conventional family life, day care has become a political issue. As pressures for federal- or state-supported day care increase, particularly in communities with many one-parent families and low-wage earners, opposition also has intensified, and community polarization has occurred—frequently to the detriment (because fiscal struggles tend to be inhibiting) of prospering, imaginative, efficiently administered centers.

Roughly speaking, day-care centers seem to fall into one of two categories: *groovy* and *custodial*.

Groovy day-care centers spring from grass-roots energy, starting with a few families, then adding more. They learn through trial and error.

Groovy centers rarely start with much equipment, so they often look shabby. They quickly perceive that children and disarray are inextricably intertwined, and so seek to *control* mess and disorder rather than *prohibit* them. Because these centers don't intend to make a profit, they learn how to spend money so that it will benefit the children rather than the adults. Aware that they don't enjoy even their own children for nine-hour stretches, the parents who run these centers don't expect to hire teachers who will "do it for the money." Because they want a homey atmosphere, and conscientious child care, these parents take an active part in running the center, rather than simply using it as a daily drop point for their children.

People, of course, make the crucial difference at these centers. The staff, young or old, wear clothes that are machine washable, suitable for floor play, and allow all varieties of sticky human contact. These staffers tend to be "huggers," conspicuously relaxed about lines of authority, power status, or other social protocols. They talk to children the way they talk to grown-ups . . . straight.

The kids walk around as if they know where they are going. If a stranger walks in and asks, "What are you doing, little girl?" the answer is likely to be direct and spontaneous. Children seem to acquire, very quickly, a sense of the group that suggests family intimacy. Children in groovy centers I visited seem to know each other's hang-ups and be philosophical about them. "Oh, don't mind him. He always plays with that truck that way," one three-year-old told me as I looked strangely at another small boy pushing a dump truck upside down across a carpet.

Groovy centers are seductive places. When you arrive with your child, you feel like hanging around awhile. The staff tends to be open, chatty, and responsive to your interest and engagement as a parent.

Custodial centers seemed more boring, by comparison. At several I visited, children were herded around with deadpan seriousness, as if the function of the center was to keep them clean, healthy, and unharmed. The staff talked respectfully to grown-ups and patronizingly to children. Their clothes were relatively formal, in the style of office workers. Staff members were scrupulously groomed, and stood up a lot, as if to emphasize their distance from the children left in their care.

Custodial centers seem to like to organize things, especially "activities" or "projects" involving the whole group. They tend to take pride in craftsmanlike results (such as the seventy-five well-glazed ashtrays I saw at one center). Some custodial centers have treasured theories of early childhood education, while others scorn theories and "treat the kids just like I would my own," a posture that ordinarily means "I don't put up with any nonsense."

Children in custodial centers may become boring themselves after a while. Most are biding their time until they can get out. They walk around looking a little lost. Some make trouble, to shake everybody up for a while; others cave in and weep. Most of them, though, wait for instructions and directions. Occasionally a really solid child will create a world of play quite exclusive of what else is happening, and absorb whatever attention comes his way.

Most parents who see a custodial center in action are turned off day care for the rest of their lives. But others seem blissfully ignorant of what goes on because they have little contact with groups of young children. A clean and orderly playroom adjacent to a modern kitchen can fool parents desperate for child care.

That good day-care centers are the result of hard work on the part of the families involved may explain why they are such a rare commodity. Hard-working parents have to want that kind of child care badly to make sure it flourishes. They have to feel it's a good thing, a positive way to bring up children. That can be very difficult in a society where institutional care of healthy children is an oddity, and a supporting body of professional literature is virtually unknown. Most magazine or newspaper articles on the subject prolong the debate over whether or not day care is good for children. Few of these articles attempt to distinguish between the varieties of day care available, and so fail to draw attention to the mechanics and motivation of centers that work most successfully.

Day-care centers that become popular because of their fine, intimate, loving care of children tend to grow in size. They grow because the more children they care for, the more money they take in and the greater chance they have for survival. Even so, private grass-roots centers are constantly in need of money and are often forced to take in more children than they can handle without losing their sense of intimacy. Often they must resort to fund raising on a big-time scale, a process which may require compromises not always in the best interests of the families involved.

At their best, however, day-care centers might be one answer to a working mother's dream. A woman in New York City whose

four-year-old girl had just been admitted to an apparently first-rate
day-care center on the Upper West Side explained, "Getting in
here is more difficult than getting into Harvard, when you're
white, WASP, and have a B average from music and art. But once
you're in, it's like an insurance policy for the rest of your life.
They take kids from infancy on and once your child is old enough
to go to school, they pick the child up from public school and
bring him back to the center for an 'after school' program.
They're open from seven to seven so families can make use of
twelve-hour care for years. Most important, the kids have this
sense of extended family. They're as familiar with the center as
they are with home, and for most of them the center is a thousand
times more exciting. It's not just the equipment; it's the kids and
the staff and the parents who like the place so much they come
and eat lunch with the children."

This woman felt that the day-care center had been a source of
education for her in bringing up her child. She got advice and
ideas from an extended community. In conflict, she got support.
When her child was sick, the center kept a back-up list of helpers
who would come to her house and care for the child. "Even if I
were only able to break even financially in order to have my
daughter there," she told me, "I would do it. The center offers a
richer community life than I could ever offer her here in the city
and it offers *me* something too, in the way of friends. And I'm
able to keep my professional work."

Few centers are as large or well organized as that one, but many
do have "kindergarten" and after-school programs, a helpful answer to the current fashion in public kindergarten hours. Most
communities have kindergartens now, but sessions last only a few
hours, often ending at eleven in the morning. Even nonworking
mothers complain that this schedule is insufficient for active five-
year-olds and disruptive of anything a mother might have arranged on her own time.

Many women who use day care admit that its carefully planned
programs ease the burden of maternal guilt. Day-care centers, like
nursery schools, offer activities, trips, and continual companionship that working mothers can't duplicate. Nor can most
household help. This is especially true of women who live in
neighborhoods where most mothers are at home and do these
things on their own. One mother of three I spoke to started work

when her second child was two. She noticed that her housekeeper didn't like to go outside with the children, and also preferred not to let neighborhood kids in. "I noticed that Jimmy never got to go to the places I used to take his older brother to—like the supermarket, the fire house, the library, other people's homes. It doesn't sound like much but I got to feel guilty about it. When I was home, I also put up with a lot more mess and kid activity than my housekeeper could handle. You can't blame her. She isn't after all, his mother."

AU PAIR GIRLS

Middle-class women often experiment with live-in help, sometimes with au pair girls—young women, frequently from abroad, who come to this country, usually for a year, and who live in, typically for a small salary, plus room and board. Although this practice is illegal now—they can't get work visas—the practice still goes on. So far everyone seems to be content to look the other way.

But while an au pair may be a charming addition to many American homes, particularly for nonworking mothers who like to come and go at unscheduled hours, au pairs don't seem to provide the hard-core security and experience that working mothers must depend on. For one thing, they are very young, which means they are likely to become involved in activities that interfere with their household duties—like getting to know other young people, and carrying on an active social life while only half-heartedly looking after their charges.

Many au pair girls have never been to this country before and working mothers may find they have an additional job on their hands familiarizing the au pair with the protocols of urban or suburban life. Many au pairs speak English poorly or not at all. Said one frustrated Maryland woman, "She told me she could *understand* English well and was learning to speak it. I didn't catch on to the fact that she couldn't do either until I noticed that she nodded up and down at my directions but then didn't do what I'd asked her to. 'Yes, yes, oui, oui,' she would nod and then disappear." This woman finally threw in the towel when she realized her au pair, who was using the family car to drive her children to school, couldn't read the traffic signs.

Many au pairs see their year abroad as high adventure and aren't automatically sensitive to the particular problems of working mothers. "I felt obligated, of course, to offer Michelle time to meet other young people, but I hadn't taken into account how hard it would be to find her companions. Many evenings I'd have to drive her somewhere so she could enjoy an evening off. It was like having another child in the family."

Once companions are found, other problems develop: "We noticed halfway through the year that Lilly was gaining weight and teased her about it. Suddenly it dawned on me that she was pregnant. But no matter what I did, she kept insisting that she was eating too much. Finally her predicament was unmistakable. After that experience I said, 'No more!'"

Au pairs tend to get homesick. "I had a girl from Denmark who cried all the time. She was the saddest creature I ever encountered, yet she insisted that everything was all right and she didn't want to go home. We tried to assure her that it was all right and we would pay for her passage to go home early. No. She would smile wanly and do her work. But I couldn't stand coming home to this girl crying all the time. We would get up for breakfast and down she would come with red swollen eyes as if she had been up all night crying. The kids treated her like a lost fawn and were taking care of her more than the reverse. After four months I couldn't take it any longer—our household was morose. So I made her go back. After that I switched to a grandmother type who arrived at eight every morning—cheerfully."

Still another handicap in the use of imported au pair girls is the problem of changeover. As soon as her visa is up, a year's worth of domestic adjustment disappears via Pan Am. Aside from the fatiguing prospect of starting all over with a new orientation program, many women feel it is hard on the children to form attachments, then have them broken, and attempt to adjust, repeatedly, to a changing of the guard.

Moreover, families disappointed in their au pair girls find it's not easy to fire or retire them. In most cases, the au pair has a one-year contract that, if broken, requires a settlement as well as return air fare.

Although au pair girls are supposedly "screened" before they are sent to America, problems of geography inhibit any opportunity for a personal interview—and thus the chance for each part to weigh the intangibles. If the girl is more comfortable with tube aluminum, vinyl upholstery, and lacquered tile floors, she may flip at the sight of your helplessly chaotic Victorian frame, complete with wide oak flooring, slate sinks, the picturesque gas lamps. Not to mention your plain-spoken, rough-and-tumble three-year-old. Call it a $350 blind date, give or take a few hundred for extras.

HOUSEKEEPERS/BABY-SITTERS

Most working mothers need and want more than a high-risk foreign-exchange adventure for household help. They need someone mature, reliable, self-sufficient, cheerful, and hard-working. A good wife, as one woman wryly put it. A grandmother, said another.

Grandmothers, alas, prove to be an expensive commodity, especially if you want one healthy enough to carry a two-year-old up the stairs, or struggle through an unwilling diaper change. In metropolitan areas this kind of help can cost $125 a week or much more. Although suburban women often find mature reliable women for less—$90 a week is considered fair—they frequently have to add on the cost of transportation and meals.

This is high-class housekeeping help, feasible only for women earning good salaries. Women who find and keep full-time housekeepers usually have full-time careers. They're not working "just to get out of the house." They usually have well-established positions or professional skills that provide them with long-range goals and commitments. They can afford to pay social security benefits, give paid vacations every year, and conscientiously allot cost of living raises. They are, moreover, likely to insist on these benefits in the name of professional solidarity even if the women they hire care little about such refinements.

"I see myself as responsible for our housekeeper's future just as I expect my company to be mindful of my own," a forty-five-year-old mother of four told me. "But it took me some time to convince her of that. She didn't want social security taken out of her salary and I had to insist on it, adjusting the salary accordingly so that she didn't feel she was being cheated. Even then it took a long time to get her to understand that is was for *her* benefit. She was quite simply frightened of any involvement with the government. But I feel very strongly about this. My husband wouldn't think of hiring a secretary without paying social security. Why should I?"

Women who can afford full-time housekeepers who are capable of good child care usually advertise for them in their community's most respectable newspaper—the first place qualified people look for job opportunities. Advertising on supermarket bulletin boards, in neighborhood papers, or through college employment agencies rarely turns up the kind of help they're looking for.

These working mothers have come to know they must *always* insist on references and then, once they've got them, must *always* check them out, usually with a personal phone call, even if it means long distance. The cost of the call may save more than money in the long run—it may mean the difference between a child cared for by a psychotic alcoholic or by a truly sensible and sensitive adult.

Women going through this process for the first time often make the mistake of hiring a person on the basis of "gut reaction." They *like* the person they are interviewing—an important ingredient, to be sure, but only one of many. Many mothers say the best way to judge a nurse or housekeeper is to have him or her work in the house for at least a weekend, interacting with their children, then watching for signs of practicality, sensitivity, and warmth.

Sometimes compromises have to be made—some qualities are more important than others. A working mother and her husband may hate smoke, smokers, and smoking, for instance, but a forty-five-year-old woman who loves children, knows how to keep a house well organized and clean, takes pride in her work, and is perfectly capable of dealing with a rowdy four-year-old may be worth having even if she chain-smokes. A young man who doesn't mind cleaning, playing with children, doing the shopping, but freezes at the thought of any cooking more complicated than boiling an egg may be tolerable in spite of his helplessness when it comes to cooking.

Most working mothers find that if they use the same standards for their own hired help they insist on in their neighbor's they find what they need. The most important message of the women I talked with is, never, never, hire anyone out of desperation.

Many working mothers feel that housework and child care are in some measure demeaning. And many have ambivalent feelings about hiring other women to take on these chores. Professional women over forty don't seem as worried about this as younger women, but "I don't like the idea of hiring someone else to do my dirty work" is a common remark.

Most younger women can't afford to hire this kind of help *and* offer employment benefits as well. But doing it any other way produces more guilt than satisfaction. "I have a wonderful woman who comes to our house every day from 7:30 A.M. to about 6 or 6:30 P.M. She's in her fifties, widowed, and her children are all grown up and gone. She loves our children and I have it made except that I can't afford to pay her what she is worth. I'm stretching it to give her $40 a week and she does everything—the laundry, the light housekeeping, and child care. She even gets supper started before I get home. I feel very badly about her, thinking that I'm using her. I didn't ask her to do all the housework. It just sort of evolved that she started doing it because she said she might as well while she was there anyhow and she says she doesn't like to be idle. But my guilt is such that, for instance, if I feel she is not doing just what I would like with the children—say in the number of cookies she hands out, or the amount of television she might allow them on a rainy day—then I don't feel I can correct her. I'm constantly feeling that I ought to be very very nice to her. I say 'thank you' so often that at the end of the day I don't feel I'm my own person. I dream of a nice clean arrangement where I pay for what I get and get only what I pay for."

This woman was a third grade schoolteacher; her husband taught history in a high school, and they had a high mortgage in a neighborhood they had chosen for good schools even though it was slightly more expensive than they could really afford. Together they earned $18,000 a year and owned two used cars which they needed to commute in opposite directions. They had three children, two of them preschoolers. When I talked with them, inflation was starting to eat into their already tight budget, and I suspect as the cost of food has skyrocketed their situation is worse than they had ever dreamed.

ALTERNATIVES

Although continuity and centralization seem to be easier on
nuclear families, women are often forced to parcel the kids out to
other households and available institutions on a trade-off basis
which sacrifices fam-i-li-ness in order to make ends meet. Many
mothers find they have to keep a bulletin board full of schedules
just so they know where each child is at any hour of the week, a
situation compounded by the need for "backup" slots in case
something falls through.

A tiny yet growing movement is afoot that may be the answer
for working mothers who don't have a good day-care center within
reach. There seem to be a growing number of young, sensitive,
highly motivated college dropouts, young men and women who
have decided, for one reason or another, to step off the higher education track and sort out where they are going and why. The Boston area, for instance, is full of colleges and also has an endless
supply of young people who want to stay in the city, but off the
campuses, at least for a while. College dropouts who are "into
children," and are looking for either board and room or just
enough money to live communally with other young people, have
taken on the au pair role in many homes.

These young people are sometimes barely a half generation
removed from the parents who employ them. They are knowledgeable about American family needs and style and know how to
get around in a city with either public or private transportation.
They'll take a group of children to a museum, play Monopoly
with a ten-year-old on a rainy afternoon, make organic bread with
a toddler, dust with one eye shut, and provide generally energetic
support to a family that isn't resolutely committed to the traditional patterns of household help.

Many metropolitan working mothers have found these young
people through advertisements in counter-culture newspapers or
bulletin boards. "I put one ad in the *Phoenix* and got over fifty
applicants," a Cambridge, Massachusetts, woman told me. "The
young woman I chose is fantastic. She comes when the children
are home, and the rest of the time she takes courses in an adult
education center or visits with her friends. She wouldn't think of
using a car when a bike or bus is available, and she gets around

better than I do. My kids, whom I used to have watched in a
fenced-in backyard, make it to the local stores now and through
her have met other kids in the area. Television is a bad word in
our house now."

Still another strategy has been used by young mothers with
preschool children who have found no day-care centers available
to them either because of geography or oversubscription. Or
because even though a good nursery school program is available in
the morning, afternoons remain a problem.

Some of these mothers form small afternoon playgroups for
their children and two or three other children of roughly the same
age; they hire a "teacher" and split the cost among the parents.
The arrangement provides a good many bonuses for the children
involved. If, for example, the children go to the same preschool,
this extra bond fortifies the school relationship. Traveling en
troupe, their two or three "best friends" become, as time goes on,
members of a special daytime extended family. Playgroups usually
rotate among children's homes so that each child can feel his
home is an essential ingredient in the mix.

The mothers who arrange the playgroups often become friends,
and the families involved may extend their relationships into
other social weekend activities. So the kids feel more and more at
home with each other and with each other's families and homes.
These child-care arrangements often provide secure, comforting,
play-filled days.

Whatever arrangement parents come up with, the concensus is
that institutional child care is far and away the best solution.
Women with very young children want them to play with other
children their own age, preferably under supervision.

Middle-class mothers who can afford "baby nurses" or full-time
housekeeper/sitters admit that they keep them on for the security
they offer rather than the developmental benefit they offer
children.

One New York executive who had her only child when she was
in her early thirties and well into her own career discovered this
problem as her baby crept out of the early infant stage into
toddlerhood.

"In the beginning, when I went back to work, Sam didn't
change my life at all . . . because I was very confident in this
nurse I had. I was working a four-day week, staying home one day,

the nurse's day off. Because he slept most of the time, I got vast amounts of work done. The nurse slept in his room, had actually taken care of *me* in the first few years of my life. She knew a lot more about babies than I did. She stayed in his room for a year and a half. Then I decided she was too old, that I needed someone more lively. So I hired a very nice girl and Sam took an instant dislike to her. He would scream whenever she came into the room.

"So back came the old nurse. She stayed for another year. But I was getting a bit fed up with her because she babied Sam incredibly. Sam was turning out to be a lot brighter than she was. She would feed him at an age when he really should have been feeding himself. She would dump too much sugar into his cereal and I would say, 'Don't do that,' and I would say, 'Don't give him a bottle, give him a cup.'

"So again during the summer I found a younger girl and she was a total disaster. Sam was in a really distressful state, sleeping poorly, crying when I left, throwing up in his bed. So back came the old nurse. I felt Sam was showing me he needed some continuity, someone he could trust. He really loves her a lot, and she loves him. So I thought, better that he should be babied than distressed.

"But, alas, I got peeved again. She was still babying him. She would give him cookies in the middle of the day and he has always been a lousy eater. I'd say, 'No, nothing in between meals, wait for lunch, give him lunch, if he's hungry, he'll really eat then.' But she would always give him cookies. And I would say, 'It's OK if he watches 'Sesame Street,' but that's it.' I would come home and Sam would tell me, 'Nanny told me not to tell you that I watched 'Batman' on T.V.' Things like that.

"So the thing that has changed my life is this constant pressure of finding help. So that if you don't want to go home at six o'clock, you can go out without feeling your child is so miserable, or needs you so badly."

Cookies and television seem to be the two great weaknesses of full-time housekeepers. They pose a more serious threat to child care than would appear at first glance. Cookies and television are child pacifiers, substitute baby-sitters, bad answers to bored kids. A steady diet of animal crackers, Fruitloops, potato chips, and Cheese Twisties is also poor nutrition. Moreover, for children from eighteen months to eighteen years, they become a "be quiet and eat some of this stuff" answer to the need for constructive and imaginative play. Television encourages demands for these snacks through advertising and periodic boredom.

Whether or not parents take either problem seriously, what cookies and television are replacing *ought* to be taken seriously. They take the place of healthy, aggressive, imaginative play, or as Urie Bronfenbrenner, Cornell University early childhood specialist puts it, "good old-fashioned family life." The answer seems to lie in some sort of group or institutional child care for children as young as one or as old as ten.

This indicates that more grade schools should have organized and supervised after-school programs, and that parents should lobby for them. It means that more nursery schools, day-care centers, and small playgroups will have to be organized, and soon. Parents will have to lobby for them and work hard to keep them going.

Getting good child care in America seems a potluck affair. Women who have found something that works talk about it in whispers. "I'm just so lucky," one woman after another uttered, gesturing madly to express the fear that something might disturb the status quo.

Many more women, however, are not lucky at all. They go from one bad housekeeper to another or rely on people they don't want to rely on because they have to. They yearn for a clear conscience. Denied it, they are often bitter. But as one black woman said, "Women aren't angry enough yet. When they are, they'll get what they want." But only if they know what they want and that seems a long time off.

eight

HOUSEWORK

The International Labor Organization has called on husbands to shoulder a bigger share of the household chores as one way to ease the burden carried by married women who work. The organization . . . says that overworked wives are a "serious problem" the world over. Studies have shown, the agency reports, that working mothers have less than two-thirds the free time enjoyed by their husbands.

"A more equitable sharing of the burden of housework and the care of children between men and women" is one approach to the problem of the overworked wife, the agency says. The New York Times, January 6, 1975

Working mothers, the common myth has it, are nettled by housework. This myth assumes that working mothers are forever bustling about trying to keep a perfect house, cook inventive meals, prepare a living room with each corner and cushion ready for the *House & Garden* photographer. The myth also assumes that because they are trying to do these things all the time, housework is one of the big bugaboos in every working mother's life.

My interviews indicate that this simply is not so. Getting housework done seems often the least important problem working mothers must confront. Many of them regard housework the same way they think about doing the filing at an office—it's a bore, but it's got to be done, so let's do it, somehow, so we can enjoy the satisfaction of a clean house.

Not every woman, of course, can put housework in its place, but I was surprised at how many women do. Whether a family kept its house neat, clean, and orderly; neat, dirty, and orderly; clean, cluttered, and disorganized—the style that kept everybody happy was usually the product of a series of compromises and an examination of priorities.

The pattern of this housekeeping style is less important in the lives of most working parents than an *attitude* toward housework, an attitude that can take on political dimensions.

"With my husband and me," said a woman from Cincinnati, "housework has become a highly sensitive issue. The only house-keeper we ever had was a white woman, and we developed one of these half-friendship, half-counseling relationships. I let her totally take over my house. And it was uncomfortable. We had deliberately moved into a mixed neighborhood and wanted our kids to have a good experience with black children. We felt that to have a black woman in the house doing housework would strengthen one of the stereotypes we were trying to avoid.

"Also, because my husband was so flexible about sharing almost anything, it was hard for him to feel that we had much need. And then, when I was little, we had maids, and I never liked the way my mother treated them or related to them."

Although this woman is in her mid-forties, she speaks for a lot of younger working mothers. These women, many of whom have been spurred on by feminist literature, regard housework as a family affair. They find the idea of hiring someone to clean their house repugnant and exploitative. They feel responsible for taking care of their own homes, and insist that their families share in that responsibility.

"I'm very uncomfortable in a position of domestic superiority," one woman said. "I feel very guilty about it. And I really don't mind housework so much. Sometimes I find I get a lot of pleasure out of doing some very specific, uncomplicated task. My husband does too. Sometimes we'll spend a whole Saturday working together. He enjoys doing dishes. His head is free to wander and he works very slowly as a result. We've never been compulsive housekeepers, and at times the house has been very messy and we've lived with it. We never got into the suburban perfect house."

Many men make the discovery that doing things around the

house, even cooking, can be fun. Busy professional men who lead very competitive lives at work may enjoy the satisfaction of doing something as uncomplicated as the laundry or taking care of a kitchen.

"Being home and working around the house is often a lot of fun," one university professor told me. He was in his second marriage, this time to a full-time university administrator.

"I've always liked to cook and I'd like to do more of it. In my first marriage, my wife wouldn't exactly say it, but you could tell sometimes that she would prefer it if I *didn't* cook. I made a big deal out of cooking, made bread and so on. Then I got into budgeting, food planning, and so on. Not very much, but enough to bother her.

"Now with Ann [his second wife], I do maybe half of what has to be done. Sometimes I'll do *all* the cooking, but also some of the organization and planning. I don't like drudgery. I'm utterly bored with cleaning. If I make a mess, I'll clean it up but I hate to clean floors.

"Part of our principle, and it works pretty well, is whoever wants to do something does it. If you don't want to clean, you both wait until one person can't stand it any more. I'm much more likely to do the dishes, for example, when they're piled up. Because I get so I can't stand that and also because I really don't mind doing them. Ann is much more likely to wash a floor. I don't think she likes to but somehow or other she goes at it like she gets something out of it.

"When I work at home, I generally find some kind of housework that has to be done. It takes an hour in our house just to water the plants every day. Or something or other has to be fixed. I'm the one who does the laundry most often, and Ann does the floors.

"We don't have as much conflict over things we don't want to do as we seem to have with the things we both like doing, like the cooking. I'm getting over it now, but at first, and for quite a long time, and still to some extent, I really don't like anybody else to be messing with the meal I'm fixing. Now we've got so that I'm better at sharing and she knows that she has to be careful. If she's going to help, she has to sort of clear it."

Most women, I've discovered, have developed a similar perspective on housework, a sense of humor about it, that enables them to put up with never-finished chores, a perpetually filled laundry basket, and overflowing ironing boards.

I did find a lot of couples who, like the couple mentioned, want to share housekeeping as part of living together, who see housework as something to be worked into a relationship. Most often these couples are young, college educated with preschool children. Most of them wouldn't dream of spending money on household "services." So restructuring housewifery roles is a way of solving problems that have to be faced.

Just as many women, however, know they'd never persuade their husbands to help with housework and they seek relief through services. Few of these women want to make a political issue out of housework, but even if they did, they can see that the deck is loaded against them, and so they seek hired help rather than risk a no-win confrontation.

Those who can afford domestic help often discover that finding and keeping good house cleaners can be time consuming and complicated by problems of diplomacy and self-consciousness.

"I found I was always chasing after help," one woman said. "I had to keep a running check on everyone, pick them up at bus stops, get home in time to pay them, keep on top of their work so I could praise where praise was called for, correct where it was not, and so on. It was a bore, and it was draining. I simply don't have time in my schedule to do that."

So what's the solution? Many women who don't want to or can't get their families to help with the housework hire professional cleaners. These companies send out men, usually two at a time, with their own cleaning materials and tools. They work (for tremendous fees) like demons. What two men can do in an hour with industrial vacuum cleaners and polishers would astonish most housewives. Many women who balk at hiring women to clean their houses have no difficulty hiring *men* to do the work.

I have tried all of the above. There was a point in my life when I did all the housework myself (first few years of marriage). I did it because I assumed that is what I was supposed to do, and I strongly discouraged my husband from interfering with these responsibilities.

Years later, pregnant with a second child, I moved into a new housekeeping phase. I hired a "cleaning lady." She took one look at me, sized me up immediately, and told me it would take her all day just to get the bathroom clean (at $25 a day), and she was right. It did. I took care of this woman for eighteen months. I waited to pick her up, in my station wagon, while my first child did everything an impatient baby does. I drove her home if it rained. I fixed her lunches. I gave her brother-in-law all our never-to-be-read books, our old clothes, our almost fixed television set, and my husband's tuxedo. I called her when she didn't show up to see if she was well. On the last day she worked for me, I vacuumed the living-room floor because she had a back problem, and although I had one too, I knew exactly what she was going through and I couldn't wish it on a friend. She still calls me for references.

I did not fire her. She quit.

I then moved into my next phase. Too broke to get another cleaning lady, I allowed my husband to help. He took over several big items. I don't remember ever asking him and if pressed I would have to admit that maybe he *always* did some things. But I allowed him back into the kitchen. Not before dinner. Just afterward, to clean up.

My third phase came with my third baby. Everything started to happen at once after this third child was born. Within a week I became a working mother, my husband had to take over almost all of the housework (because I also got sick), and within a month I had joined a women's consciousness-raising group. That's when housework became politicized in our household. I refused to say thank you when he did the dishes. I refused to say thank you when he did anything but pass the butter. We divided up our Saturdays into domestic duty blocks—he did all the bathrooms and the children's rooms, I did the rest, except for the basement, which I no longer had to look at (if I didn't want to). He made the breakfasts, I made the dinners, and we all ate out at lunch. He cleaned up the dinner dishes; I cleaned up the breakfast dishes. I mowed the lawn. He clipped the hedges and raked the leaves. He did the shopping. I did the spending. (Don't ask.)

This lasted for a while but we grew tired. Both of us. And at some point we noticed that the house was dirty again. Never a very active political force myself, I started to thank him again—for just about anything. All he had to do was put his shoes in his closet and I thanked him.

Then I discovered a cleaning company. I called one advertised on the radio and out came *two men*, at eight in the morning, with huge vacuum cleaners, floor waxers, buffers, wood cleaners. They

spent eight hours there. It cost me $140. They promised me it
would take them only two or three hours to do it next time.
Terrific. I signed them up and back they came a month later. It
cost me $51.

On the third visit, having told everyone how I had discovered
the way to beat the working mother's cleaning problems—how the
political and moral women could stop worrying about exploiting a
cleaning lady, how the ineffectual women could stop catering to a
cleaning lady, how the frantic women could stop catering to a
house, and how the guilty women could be cleansed (they'd have
a clean house and save money)—I made this other discovery
about the cleaning companies.

I discovered that the cleaning companies exploit the men. They
got $.20 out of every dollar I paid the company. They were
allowed no lunch break—had to go from job to job all day. They
were paid only for days they worked—no sick leave. They were paid
only for hours they were sent out on jobs—if the company didn't
have enough work, no paycheck. They were paid, consequently,
less than the cleaning ladies, and got none of the care they might
have commanded in a more relaxed circumstance.

Are we to stop exploiting women only to exploit men? I asked
myself.

So I guess I wind up being all for families cleaning their own
homes.

And while housework doesn't have to be blown into a major
problem, it also has to get done—with greater or lesser scrupulous-
ness depending on family concensus. It seems from my interviews
that many husbands and wives work out the equation in a variety
of ways, seizing upon each other's strengths, tolerances, and areas
of strong preference. But some men need a push, and some expect
instruction. It seems that a working mother who wants to preserve her sanity—and hasn't a troupe of housekeepers to handle
the job—better insist that housekeeping chores be approached in
a spirit of parity.

Few husbands seem to mind all that much, once they develop
confidence that they know what they're doing. And, as discussed
in earlier chapters, no serious harm can befall a young son or
daughter obliged to make a bed or swab out a bathroom. And that
son or daughter is learning habits that will be hard to shake
twenty years from now, when he or she is working out similar
problems in adult life.

nine

COPING

A teacher who instructed college students in her child development class that breast-feeding is a beautiful experience has been suspended by the college for practicing what she preached. . . . She used to breast-feed the baby . . . in the woman's faculty lounge between classes. She finally had to resort to sneaking the child into the rest room of a nearby filling station when the college's board of trustees passed a regulation barring the children of employees from campus during working hours. . . . The President of the college said he feared it would set a bad precedent. . . . The feeling was that such employes as secretaries, clerks and cleaning women might desert their duties to breast-feed and that the efficiency of the school would suffer.
The New York *Times*, January 20, 1975

"How do you cope with it all?" That's the question just about all working mothers are asked sooner or later as—and when—they manage the two main aspects of their lives with seeming grace and good humor. Every woman I talked with had her own techniques, of course, and each one had specific problems that are more or less her own. But the infinite variety of problems and solutions might nonetheless be roughly summarized, at least in a general way.

Of the less predictable issues that confront the family of a working mother, one of the most important may be, oddly enough, where to *live*—where to live in relation to husband's job, wife's job, school, shopping facilities, a commuter facility, pediatrician's office, dentist's office, a YMCA, bank, church, or any other facility or institution important to that family's life.

Working mothers with the luxury of foresight and careful planning have found that a house or apartment chosen with the above factors in mind reduces "coping" problems considerably.

A home near good schools and other community facilities is usually easy to find, but a home that will accommodate the jobs of *both* husband and wife is more difficult to locate. Few couples seem to choose a homesite with the husband's commuter time chiefly in mind. Or, if commuting time *is* considered, suburban life is chosen anyway, so that weekends can be spent "in the country." Gardening and hiking are possible, and the gritty truths of city life—such overcrowded schools and restricted after-school play space—can be avoided.

Living in the country and working in the city is fine as long as only one parent is doing it, at least for those who like it. But when two parents are an hour away from their children, problems are bound to occur.

So what's a couple to do? Obviously some compromises have to be made, and the choice may prove crucial. One group of women I interviewed worked at the same place—a fair-sized university—but lived in vastly different areas. The university town was on a number of highway routes, offered inexpensive and convenient public transportation to the inner city, was on the outskirts of a major eastern metropolitan area, and had first-rate public schools. The women I interviewed were either professors or administrators at the college. All had young children.

One woman, a tenured professor of sociology, with two boys aged five and eight, lived on the outskirts of the college campus. Her husband was a doctor. Before the birth of their children they had lived in the city and she had driven to the university each day.

"We loved the intensity of city life. Both of us were brought up in New York City and are comfortable with the mood. Then we had our first child.

"Just before the baby was born, we started talking about how life would be for me, with a child to care for and my work as well. We decided, finally, that we had to move. I could see that it made more sense for me to be close to the baby when I was working than it was for my husband. I wanted to nurse, and obviously it would have been impossible if my job were an hour away.

"So after the baby was born, we bought a house near the university and my husband commutes into town. This is a burden on both of us in a way. He has a long commute, I miss the shops, feel out of things and isolated. But I couldn't manage the children and the household any other way. My husband makes some compromises too. He gets up at 5:30 every morning in order to see his first patients at 7:00 and be home by 5:30 in the evening."

This woman went on to mention some of the social differences her arrangement made for her and her husband.

"Many of the people who live here are associated with the university and that means that *my* colleagues, for the most part, are more available to us socially than my husband's. Evenings of shop talk with my colleagues are often a bore for him, and he may turn boorish, which means we often end an evening with an unpleasant rehash of 'the problem.' *His* colleagues, all doctors, tend to be married to nonworking mothers, and we don't always have a lot in common. So, socially we do seem to struggle. Still, the children go to good schools, have lots of friends in the neighborhood—a comfort to me when I'm away—and they benefit from a lot of university events and facilities."

By contrast, one of this woman's colleagues made a different decision—perhaps underestimating the importance of location and so inviting problems, still to be resolved. A professor of fine arts, she was married to a stockbroker. She and her husband wanted to live in the country—not suburbia. So they moved farther out and bought a house with a barn and some land for a garden. The husband commuted an hour and fifteen minutes each way (in good traffic) and she was about forty minutes from her campus office.

"We love our house, but as the children get older I'm beginning to see that maybe we've got ourselves a problem. My children, for example, are old enough now to want an independent social life, yet they live too far from most families to get there on their own. I don't mind the commute in good weather, but in the winter I am fearful of driving in snow and ice so a lot of the time I'm nervous, dreading, every morning, the weather and the drive. My husband, who loves the farm the most, is on it the least. His hours are longer than mine and his commute means he gets home that much later than I do. My baby-sitter, on the other hand, is a blessing. If she leaves me, I don't know how I would find another one like her.

"I miss out on a lot of social life at the university—I don't mean parties, but concerts, lectures, family gatherings. I've felt for some time that we ought to move closer to the university but we're married to a house, it seems, as much as we're married to each other. If we lived near campus, for example, my youngest could go to the university nursery school, one of the best around, but I have no way of getting her home at noon so she doesn't get nursery school."

Still another professor at the college lived in the city forty minutes away from the college with her four-year-old child and her husband, a free-lance consultant with generally more flexible hours. When he was working, however, he was on the road or working through the night, rarely available for child care. Although the wife's hours were long too, and predictable, they were also fairly rigid, and she found that their living arrangement was beginning to present problems.

"When my husband is available, everything works out well. He can be there to supervise the connections between nursery school and baby-sitter and afternoon shifts. But when he isn't I feel a lot of pressure. I leave at 7:30 each morning, a half hour before my daughter leaves for school. If my husband is gone, this means finding a friend to leave her with. If something goes wrong, I'm pressed to find ways to get to her or find substitute help. We love city life, my husband especially doesn't want to give it up, but because *my* hours are stable, it often occurs to me that it would make sense to live nearer my job. Our problem, I guess, is that we bought our house and fixed it up before we had our child. We have an investment in the house and we love it. I'm hoping that as my daughter gets older, the situation will improve."

Unfortunately, the situation tends to become more rather than less complex. As children grow older, and wish for more independence, parents often worry about leaving them unsupervised. Moreover, and in spite of that appetite for independence, many children are visibly shaky when left too long to their own devices, particularly when parents are known to be some distance away.

The question of "where to live" affects more than parent/child availability. For many working couples, proximity to shopping, business, and other services proved equally important. Having "everything nearby" simplified their busy lives. One woman I spoke with switched pediatricians, dentists, and banks in order to use the nearest—in this case neighborhood—services. Her children could walk to their doctor and dentist. She used a local bank's "night drop," or Saturday morning hours. A local supermarket delivered their groceries, and a family shoe store was only three blocks away.

When husband and wife work in different towns, most families arrange to live nearer the wife's job. This arrangement usually works relatively well, although it also puts the burden of childrearing where it usually is, with the wife/mother. If a man's job is less demanding, more flexible, or his position is such that he can take an afternoon off without feeling accountable to someone for it, the family might situate nearer the husband's job. Women, ironically, often have less flexible job situations, and badly need that kind of support.

The home site also affects the kind of child care or other household help available, and many women are coming to choose communities that offer the most opportunities for good help. Public transportation, of course, becomes an important consideration.

Many women have learned to choose a neighborhood before they choose a house or apartment. They look for other children on the street. "If a kid doesn't have friends to play with during the days," one woman said, "he'll come home and watch television. If your kids have a busy neighborhood, a suitable baby-sitter will be easier to find. After all, you don't need Wonder Woman there, if the kids are outside playing with friends."

Other children, and recreation facilities, are even more important during the summer months. Some women find out about the summer day-camp situation even before they look for a real estate agent.

Another important question working parents must cope with is "what to eliminate from their lives." What activities, events, recreations, or privileges must working mothers give up? What do their husbands give up? And what kinds of things are least essential, the first to go?

Facing this inevitable paring down head-on instead of just letting things happen can make the lives of working parents much easier. The decision to cut out Thursday night bridge club, or Friday night dinner parties, or all weekday cocktail parties, or tennis on Saturday and Sunday afternoons may eliminate recurring quarrels over who is entitled to what, and when.

Couples who can discuss what's important to them and what's not stand a better chance of holding onto their real pleasures. Some start out with major cutbacks, then gradually restore sacrificed pleasure activities as they adjust to their schedules. This is easier for couples with new babies—cutting back comes more naturally then. But for families with a mother returning to work the adjustment is difficult. Many husbands, faced by sudden and drastic changes, feel that their wives' working is exacting too stiff a price, eliminating a number of favorite recreations, in addition to imposing upon the family a busier schedule and a less efficient household.

As one husband put it, "When my wife went back to work, we all expected to put out more, but the pressure got to me. I felt guilty about taking a Saturday to play golf, something I used to do a lot, and I resented having to give it up. It wasn't that she *tried* to make me feel guilty. It was just that whenever I left or planned to leave, I was aware of all the things that I could be doing in the house. It was a bad situation. In fact, it still is."

Another husband admitted that some of these adjustment changes are exaggerated in everyone's mind because they seem so permanent—even when concessions are only temporary.

"When we had our first baby, Lily wanted to nurse him and still work. Before the baby she had taken public transportation and I had taken the car. Then all of a sudden she needed the car in order to get home for a midday nursing. That was all right. I understood that. But the next thing I knew a lot of other things were changing too. Her nursing seemed to affect our cocktail hours, our dinner times, our social life, and she was always tired. At the end of three months I'd built up a pretty good case of resentment. I hardly ever got to do anything with the baby, who always seemed to be nursing, and my wife was either working or tending to that baby.

"After the third month, things got better. Lily wasn't so tired. The baby got on a better schedule. We started sleeping through the nights and we could stay away from the house longer than two hours on a Saturday evening. Needless to say, if someone had explained this to me earlier, I'd have relaxed a bit."

Husbands, however, aren't the only ones who have to give up

some things. Women who try to do too much stretch themselves too thin, and are certain to lose out on their own leisure activities.

Several women told me that they were determined to keep up with their community and school obligations, which often meant evening meetings or committee work on top of their jobs. They were also determined to spend a lot of time with their children, "be there" for their husbands, and keep the household running smoothly. Their schedules, they found, were so crammed they often had to give up "frills," like physical exercise or long-treasured hobbies. Though they were meeting all their commitments, they were losing an important source of refueling. Eventually, they grew frantic.

"I was obviously doing too much but I'm full of energy and I was very determined. Gradually, however, my moods became angry moods, and instead of taking my fatigue out on strangers, I took it home with me. I began to feel a failure. I didn't have any time left for myself. More important, I thought if I complained, that meant I'd have to quit. So I kept it up until one day at the office I broke down and cried over some silly thing. I called my doctor for a tranquilizer and he called me in for a physical. When I told him what was happening to me, he gave me a lecture, and, sure enough, told me to quit my job. That was the first time I sat down and asked myself what was really important to me. I decided my job was more important than the antiwar movement. I decided it was more important to be with my children pleasantly than to lobby for a new school building and organize the school circus. So I quit a lot of activities and took up tennis. I felt guilty for a long time about the war and my tennis but I got over it and things are better since I made the change."

Most women have had to give up, entirely, activities on weekday evenings. Friday evenings, many families found, were also a problem. Women, more so than men, said they were tired by then and would rather curl up with a book, watch some television, and "baby-sit" for their children than go out. "Friday night is when I want my husband to come home with Colonel Sanders chicken and tell me to relax," a nurse told me. "I'm on my feet all week. By Friday I want to put them up in my own living room."

Working fathers, however, often had a different concept of relaxation in mind. One told me, "I want to go out on Fridays and my wife hates to. I just like to socialize some, have a couple of drinks, go to a Chinese restaurant—unwind a bit. So we compromise. If I call the baby-sitter, take care of the kids' supper, make all the arrangements, and just ask my wife to drift along, she'll go. But she says it's too much effort to handle the logistics. It's not worth it to her. That's okay with me. A couple of times she's told me to go myself—to a movie or with some friends. But I want her along."

When working mothers give dinner parties they claim they keep things simple and small. Some gave one or two big parties a year, "to get everyone paid off at once." Others, many others, simply stop the process altogether. "We're more apt to go out to dinner with another couple or by ourselves as entertainment," many women said. "If we want to take time off socially we'd rather sit down and have someone wait on us than the other way around, and once you stop giving dinner parties, miraculously you stop getting invited to many."

Social activities for most of these families consist of things everyone in the family can take part in. "We like to watch football," one couple told me. "But since I started working, we invite other families with children over to cook pizza in the kitchen or something and watch the game over our shoulders. That way our children get to play with other kids, don't feel neglected, and we get some of our own fun in at the same time."

Sometimes couples found they could maintain favored recreational activities if they made accommodations for children in the process. "I like to play basketball every Sunday morning," one husband told me. "But after my wife went to work, she told me she thought I ought to stay home and do something with the family. She pointed out that by the time I get home, shower, and catch my breath, it's after lunchtime. She'd had the kids all morning and couldn't do any of her own work. Some other fathers had the same problem, so we rented a gym with play space for the kids. I take the kids with me; they play in the gym, my wife gets some extra rest and enjoys reading the Sunday paper with a quiet cup of coffee. I get to play basketball, the kids get to roughhouse in the gym, and my wife has a quiet morning to herself."

Whatever a couple "gives up" seems to be less important than the conscious planning of schedules and priorities. Drifting into unexamined routines, sacrificing treasured activities, responding more and more on a crisis basis as family pressures mount may lead to unexpected dangers. Both husbands and wives need moments of privacy, the chance to keep in touch with a secret life of one's own. The treadmill that working mothers face is so complicated and full of constant activity that they need, periodically, to escape it altogether.

"If anything, my working has brought us closer together, because we have so little free time. We don't entertain much. We use our weekends to be together and do things that have to be done for the family or household." Women said that over and over.

Free time can be gobbled up in togetherness.

Many working mothers know what they are missing in life and they fantasize about getting it . . . because they used to have it. Private leisure time.

Another difficult coping area seemed to be supper hour. The five to eight evening shift seems a common nightmare for just about all the working mothers I talked to. Shifting gears, back into the domestic routine, is more difficult, however, for some than for others. I wondered why.

First of all, I discovered, some ingredients frequently make it harder for women. It's easier to come home to one child, for instance, who is waiting to tell you everything that happened to him than it is to come home to three or five. If a woman has a job that requires her to work sitting down at a desk all day, she may find standing up in a kitchen with the chaos of four children at her skirts a welcome change. But if she's physically tired, the transition is much more difficult.

Rattled by the first two hours at home, many women can't get over that quickly enough to make the rest of the evening pleasurable. Once they get the children to bed, they have residues of tension which carry over into relations with their husbands. If they can't find a solution to that problem, what was once an issue about "shifting gears" becomes an issue of whether or not she should work at all. And *that* issue, close to the heart of many working mothers, is a bombshell in the best of marriages.

Some women with supper-hour problems ask their baby-sitters to stay on an extra hour to ease the transition. Others arrange to have their household help start supper for them. Still others use the weekend to prepare meals in advance for the coming week.

But the real problem, of course, is the emotional shift these women must face daily, the need to sweep their minds clear of work preoccupations and embrace their children and the responsibility of family life.

This process can be made more troublesome if a woman feels her children have not been cared for well during the afternoon. Uncertain child care or maternal guilt from any source tends to take on exaggerated importance, and may condition a mother to want to "reimburse" her children the moment she walks in the door.

"By four in the afternoon I start to feel guilty," one woman told me. "So by six, when I get home, I feel some desperate pressure to show my kids I really love them. I don't feel comfortable, for example, saying no to them about anything during that first hour. Sometimes I think they sense this and take advantage of me. The worst part is that after a while I can't stand their demands any more, and I end up screaming at them for things I would normally ignore."

The ideal solution here would seem to be to erase maternal guilt altogether. Then women could walk into their homes at the end of the day and regard their children's demands with equilibrium. Barring this, however, the nearest—and most desirable—source of support is the husband.

Of the women I interviewed, a great many got home much earlier than their husbands. Sometimes this was absolutely unavoidable. Some women, for example, had taken jobs that allowed them to leave early precisely so that they could get home to their children. But occasionally I'd meet a couple who had decided that during the childrearing years they would both try to get home early from their jobs. The husbands, where it was necessary to work a longer than eight-hour day, went off early in the morning or took work home or made other professional compromises.

Husbands, of course, make the best helpers, though few that I encountered were really interested in kitchen chores. Some fathers, however, take on a major share of general child care, meeting the kids as they returned home from school or play, listening to their review of the day's activities, playing with them, or otherwise engaging them in some sort of family activity.

Getting home as soon as possible seems to be one compromise working parents need to make no matter how much help they have in the home or how old their children are. Parents in professions that occasionally involve five o'clock drink dates might suggest breakfast meetings instead, or insist on normal work-week hours.

Unfortunately, getting home early from work often runs counter to the American work ethic. Ambitious, productive, important people take pride in the endless stretching of their workday. An executive home by 5:30, in the spirit of this tradition, is an executive without drive or ambition. Unfortunately, the working father who *doesn't* get home by 5:30, or as soon as reasonably practicable, may wind up without a family, in either the literal or figurative sense. One woman I interviewed told me that she had mentioned to another couple—both doctors—that she had done something one day with her husband and kids at 5:30. The doctors expressed astonishment, asking her what time her husband got home from work. When she told them they were both home at 5:15 every day, the doctors called across the room to her husband and told him that was no way to get ahead. "Come to think of it," she said to me, "how did they think I was going to get ahead?"

Periods of unusual stress among children pose another serious concern for working mothers. Whenever a child faces a difficult stage of development, a special problem at school, or makes clear in some way that he or she is disturbed, working mothers often feel desperately vulnerable and shaky.

Many women jump immediately to the conclusion that the problem is their fault—for working. Even those who don't want to believe that suspect it anyhow. They suggest to themselves, their husbands, or their friends that they probably haven't been sufficiently available. Sometimes, of course, they are right. Few couples who work can raise children without passing through periods when they are not able to give as much time as is needed to their children.

Given that this is bound to happen sometime to almost everybody, how can working parents cope? My interviews suggest that, for most women, the first thing to do is to repress any thought that one ought to quit work. In most cases this simply makes matters worse, adding guilt and resentment to an already tense family situation. Secondly, no matter what the problem is, assume from the start that it is temporary and that, given your alert reaction to it, you're going to lick it—soon. One may need to be so armed with positive thoughts because, as one experienced woman told me, "I also learned, in two instances, that for a while at least I was going to have to put out in a big way. If a problem is serious, solutions won't be easy. A child may make inhuman demands on a working mother at times and as far as I can tell there's nothing else to do but throw yourself into the effort."

Adele had two boys, thirteen and fifteen. She was a social worker with a demanding job—head of an agency in a large community. She lived in a bedroom suburb, some forty-five minutes from her job. Her lawyer husband also worked in the city. When her youngest son was seven, Adele recalled, she noticed he was gaining weight. Within six months he had put on ten pounds. She noticed that he was more and more withdrawn at times, and then quick to cave in, cry, and get angry.

"I went to my son's school and talked with his teacher. Greg had evidently remarked to her that his parents 'never listen to me.' He didn't seem to have any close friends in his classroom and the kids were starting to tease him about his weight. In the teacher's view, he had classic symptoms of a child who felt neglected, was insecure, and was trying to compensate for 'lack of love' through food and appeals to other adults for attention.

"I felt very vulnerable, sitting there in the principal's office. The teacher knew I was gone from my home all day. I stood accused of neglect, and both teacher and principal made the typical suggestions that Greg may be feeling upset about something in the home, that he might be lonely, etc. Well, I was willing to shoulder *some* of the responsibility for Greg's condition. After all, how could I have sat back and watched him put on that weight? Why didn't I know that he was behaving strangely in his classroom? I had been busy but I also knew that that wasn't enough to send Greg into a tailspin. He was or had been a pretty solid kid and his father and I devote a lot of family time to both boys. So I couldn't believe that my not being there in the afternoons was the only problem."

Adele insisted that Greg be "observed" in his classroom by a professional child psychologist, a service she knew was available through the local schools. She told his teacher that she felt something else was bothering Greg and that although she was going to keep her eyes out at home and try to talk with him herself, she wanted feedback from someone else who could watch Greg interact with his peers without knowing that he was being watched. At the end of the observation period, Adele discovered some problems she hadn't even considered.

"Greg was ambidextrous. Both the teacher and I knew that and had expected he might have difficulty learning to read. When he proved to be able to read above his age level, we stopped worrying about it. But the psychologist observed that Greg had a lot of trouble with certain co-ordination problems—a common ambidextrous backlash. At seven, he was finding that he couldn't hold his own at recess where the boys were starting to play soccer and baseball. The other kids never picked him to be on a team and word had spread that Greg was no good at sports. He felt badly about himself. He felt so badly that he didn't want to talk about it."

Adele had started to isolate her problem but she still had hard work ahead of her. She had to turn his eating habits around; she had to find ways to help Greg feel better about himself; she had to find things that he could do well with his peers that they would value him for; and she needed to find some way to help him with his sports problems. She also had to tend to her other child, her job, her husband, and their household.

Greg was thirteen when I met Adele. She told me that it had taken two years to get Greg's weight back to normal. During that time she had sought the advice of her pediatrician, a physical therapist, and a number of professional counselors. Greg had made some progress with his physical problems but he was still shy of competitive sports. He was good at swimming, however, something she had learned many children with co-ordination problems could handle. So she and her husband made sure Greg got the chance to swim all year around.

Adele was a very competent and self-confident mother. Her professional training had helped her get the kind of advice and help she needed. She tried to bolster her son at home whenever and however she could. That meant that she had cut down on her normal social load and "spent a lot of time cooking delicious nonfattening meals."

Adele's experience underlines the difficulty working mothers face getting sound advice, particularly when it comes to childhood adjustment problems. The conventional view of working mothers —that they constitute an offense to all parental decency—is so ingrained that few experts are eager to look beyond the "self-evident" truths of the situation. This seems true of doctors and psychiatric counselors as well as teachers, particularly elementary schoolteachers, who, though many are also working mothers themselves, are often openly antagonistic toward working mothers. Some women I talked with sensed a bias more complicated than the visceral feeling that a working mother is ipso facto a neglectful mother. "When I stayed home," one woman remarked, "my children's teachers were unquestionably the 'professionals' in their lives. That position lent stature to those teachers and most of us mothers deferred to it. When I went back to work, however, I noticed a change. My youngest was in the first grade with the same teacher who had taught my two older children. I felt a competitive friction between this woman and myself whenever I had a conference with her. No doubt I was less reverent, but she seemed to me less sure of her ground."

Working mothers may have to make an extra effort to reassure the professionals who work with their children that they are just as concerned as other mothers. With teachers this may mean faithful attendance at all teacher-parent conferences or promptness in communicating concerns about issues affecting the child.

Doctors and counselors present more of a problem. Several women told me their pediatricians openly declared their disapproval of mothers working while their children were young. The assumption of this moral posture—by precisely those to whom the mothers had entrusted the medical care of their children—produced profound conflict for these parents, who found themselves having to take on a new burden of guilt or sharply reduce their sense of trust in the judgment of these doctors.

Some women whose children had serious problems had been introduced—either through social workers, doctors, or school guidance counselors—to other families who met regularly with a therapist to discuss similar problems. Sometimes just the children or one parent were involved. One woman had been asked to join a woman's group formed from mothers whose children were in therapy at a clinic. Not all of the mothers worked, but the experience was so helpful she recommended it strongly.

"I'd been feeling so guilty over my child's problems that just listening to other women talk gave me a better perspective. My daughter suffered from insomnia at age ten. I had been working only a year as a teacher and at my age [thirty-five] it's difficult to start all over again with a lot of confidence. I thought Susan's problems were the result of *my* tension. By the time I joined the women's group, I'd already learned from Susan's therapist that her insomnia was related to her bad feelings about herself because she had a lot of repressed anger. My husband and I never show any anger, as it happens, a holdover from two families where it wasn't allowed. Susan felt she was a monster for feeling 'so mean.' So she wouldn't sleep, or was afraid to go to sleep. As long as she was awake she could control the 'monster' in her.

"Knowing all this had helped, but the women I met in this group demonstrated how rapidly I was falling into another trap—as a working mother I was about to start a whole other syndrome with my kids. I had less time and patience for them, and I was about to start suppressing the feelings I had about that too."

Coping with these and other perplexing problems takes a certain philosophical detachment, what some women refer to as the need for "Norman Vincent Pealing" one's way through a crisis. Divorced or unmarried mothers have the most difficulty at these times. They can't retreat to a husband willing to reassure them. The problem, many women felt, was compounded by the need to bolster themselves in defense of the attitudes of others. It's as if they had to treat two patients at the same time—themselves and their child, when what they wanted and needed most was to resolve the problems of the child. Yet the extra time and strength needed by the child can't come from a wavering adult. So they ended up coping with two problems, one of which they resented terribly. Sometimes it became difficult to distinguish between them, making the resentment a woman felt toward those who frowned on her working arrangements mixed up with her feelings about her disturbed child.

Most women say the greatest support they get is from other working mothers. From them they get encouragement, commiseration, and the benefit of hindsight after similar experiences.

"Common sense and a soft shoulder," one woman said, "is worth much more than any therapist's couch."

Of the predictable problems a working mother must cope with, where school is concerned, none is more alarming though unavoidable than the "separation" issue, particularly where young children and a new school are concerned.

Many mothers introducing a child to nursery school or kindergarten spend a long time easing a child in—staying for half the morning, starting the child with short sessions and gradually increasing them. Six years ago, one nursery school director told me, she used to plan gradual starting sessions with only a handful of children coming for a couple of hours each day. She took three weeks to get the whole school going full steam with full attendance. Even then she invariably had a few stragglers who needed their mothers to stay much longer.

"If I did that now," this teacher told me, "I couldn't fill the school. More than half my mothers work and they can't wait for the process to finish. They need to drop their child off and run. I have to adjust that child because she can't take the time."

This period presents many young working mothers with one of their first major moments of indecision. One suburban woman told me, "It had taken me six months to get my job and set up all the arrangements for my three-year-old daughter; and then on the first week she cried and clung to me pathetically each morning I took her to what I thought was a lovely small nursery school. I nearly quit right then. I was exhausted, tense, and felt a failure. 'How do other mothers do it?' I asked myself every day."

For working mothers, getting a child adjusted to nursery school or a day-care center is not an option. It *has* to work. This often makes a mother tense just when she can least afford to be. The problem begins as she rushes to get out of the house on time, maybe adding a little extra emphasis to her pleas that the child hurry up and finish his cereal or get his shoes on. She's in a hurry. What for? the child thinks. Is she rushing to get rid of me?

Nursery school teachers claim that they can often trace a child's difficulty saying good-bye to a parent to tension in the home related to a mother's work. Family arguments over whether or not a wife should work or the conflict many mothers feel about whether or not they should work rub off on children, who become conflicted too.

Many children also seem to fear that mother is going off to some unknown territory that may be more important than or alien to the family. They cannot image what she's doing while they are confined to school, but whatever it is, their imaginations play frightening or threatening games with them.

So, what is a mother to do? The easiest problem to solve is a child's fears that his mother is disappearing. Most women find that bringing a child to visit their place of employment, perhaps several times in the course of a year, helps eliminate the problem.

"When my kids were very young, I brought them into the office one day, and when they left, they had hung little pictures and messages on the walls," one New York book-club editor explained. "I took that as a clue. They wanted me to be reminded of them during my work day. Now I bring their school pictures in and put them on my bulletin board and they love it. And frankly, it's a bonus for me on the job. Their paintings and drawings are a good reminder to the rest of the people in here that I am a working mother, and that my small children need a portion of me too."

One mother of eight, who works on an assembly line in an electrical plant, discovered that when she brought a few of her children in, they looked around for a telephone.

"They wanted to know how they could reach me and now they know—I'm only a phone call away from them. I think it's reassuring to all of them."

Women with lower echelon jobs in large corporations sometimes encounter corporation or plant resistance to such visits. Only after organized efforts are they able to win what seem to them a minor concession, an important step for them in getting the company to "humanize" their jobs.

"This place is so stuffy anyway," a secretary in a large New York law firm exclaimed, "that when I asked my boss if I could bring my two kids in for a visit one day he said 'no' without thinking. I was given a little speech about setting a bad example, being disruptive to his partners, etc. So the rest of us women met and decided to shake them up. They're so uptight about equal-employment opportunity for women now anyway that when we all made our 'request' together, they conceded. And you know, on the afternoon of the 'open house,' those men had a good time in spite of themselves."

Maternal guilt, of course, is a more difficult problem than the need to leave a child in order to get to work on time. Many women, no matter what they are feeling, what doubts, fears, or pressures, hold themselves in, deliberately appear relaxed at 7:30 in the morning when they know that within an hour they must manage the breakfast clean-up, get a child dressed, get themselves dressed, get a cantankerous car started, get a child to school (perhaps get several other children to school as well), and arrive fresh at their jobs. Once they've deposited their child in a nursery school, with a cheerful smile and a friendly kiss at the puzzle table, they hold their breaths and leave. If the child cries, they tell themselves they've done all they could. "He's got to get over it himself now."

This technique—by far the most popular—usually works, working mothers told me. Sometimes it took a week, sometimes three. But women claimed that everything worked out well if they just stuck to their guns and insisted that this was the way things were going to be. Nursery school teachers, however, disagree. Several told me that they thought this was a "short-term solution." As one director put it:

"If a mother can afford to, it is better to ease the child into school. Stay for a while and help the child get involved with the classroom so that he knows that support is there, or at least an option. Children who stop fussing 'because there's no use' try again in a few months."

Another mother compromised:

"I found I could sense when Peter was going to balk at going to school and if I couldn't coddle him that day, I left. But the next day I planned to stay anyway for just a while, perhaps to read him a story or sit down with him at some activity. Gradually he has learned that he doesn't have to test me in that way."

Another woman went one step further:

"After I had given it my best and we still had separation problems, I decided it would be easier for my daughter to say good-bye to me at home than in the school so I arranged for her to be picked up by a friend. She gets into the car for some reason without a whimper. When my friend can't pick her up, I get my husband to take her. She finds it easier to say good-bye to him than me. My way of solving this, I guess, is to avoid putting myself in that nursery school so she can do it. The teacher probably thinks I'm not facing the problem, but in my mind anything that works is okay."

The question may be whether it works best for mother or child. If one is sure things are well with the child, teachers feel, it's bound to be better for a mother too.

Many women, however, find that things don't work out well for anyone and they quit. Most often they feel that their children are suffering in some way. Either they haven't been able to find a satisfactory child-care solution or their children, for other reasons, can't make the adjustment. Fewer women quit because of a disapproving husband, although many women give up their jobs if they can't afford professional help in the home and aren't getting enough help from their husbands.

A woman who wants to hold to a demanding schedule and feel that she is doing her job well must get some measure of positive feedback from *both* of her jobs. Women who try working and then give it up often have jobs that are unsatisfying to them, for which they are overqualified and underpaid, or which provide no appreciation of their labors and problems.

Women with college degrees and several years of housewifery on their résumés often take jobs that are poorly paid and that demand few skills—as clerks, cashiers, typists, receptionists. After the first flush of freedom they feel from getting out of the house, they lose their excitement about their jobs and often have difficulty with their bosses or colleagues. They feel "used." Their tiring schedules are made more tiresome from the boredom they feel on the job. Then, as soon as they hit problems at home, they have what seems a good excuse to quit. They can speak with conviction about the impossibility or dangers of being a working mother.

Lee was thirty-eight years old and had two children, aged thirteen and eight. Before having her children she'd worked as a teacher in a private school. She had liked teaching then and wanted to return to it. Unfortunately, the teaching field was flooded, and without her certificate, something she hadn't needed in a private school, she had no chance of getting a job. So she took a job as a clerk in a fancy store that sold a lot of things she wanted for her own home. Her husband had hit a difficult time as a salesman; they needed the money; and furthermore, she felt, she could use an employees' discount to purchase furnishings they had always wanted. So she started out full of enthusiasm.

During the first six months she enjoyed herself. She lost weight, bought some rugs and curtains, and still had some money left over to help run the household. A high school girl came in after school to watch the children. As the children were in school until two every day, she was only "leaving" them for three and a half hours, she felt, and they seemed to be doing fine.

Then slowly, during the three and a half years, things started to go wrong.

"At first I loved it. It was great just getting out and seeing all the pretty things and getting dressed up. But then gradually, it stopped being fun. Standing on your feet all day in a salesroom is tiring. But we needed the money. I was making $2.25 an hour.

"In the beginning I had a pretty good baby-sitter. But then she got a job in an ice-cream parlor and I couldn't get another one. Making supper once I got home was hard. Unless you want TV dinners all the time, you have to cook on your feet, and it seemed to me that it was one meal after another, on my feet all day.

"My husband *hated* my working. The house got messy, and he likes a neat house. My husband is exhausted when he gets home. He's on his feet a lot of the time too, selling all day. So he was too tired to do housework.

"For a while I was working a late shift and he would get home before me. He would be so upset by the house. I was going through a raft of baby-sitters at the time and they would just sit down and eat ice cream and watch television.

"After a while, I let my oldest child take care of the younger one because I found him to be more reliable than the girls I could get as a baby-sitter. But they didn't like being alone and my husband would come home and see them unhappy. Finally the little bit of money I was making didn't seem to be worth it.

"One other thing. The people in the store always made me feel small. If I went to buy something on my discount, they would act as if they were doing me a big favor. At the end we had some terrible scenes. I wouldn't take any more put-downs.

"I feel better staying home. My children are pleased that I'm here when they get home. My husband is too, and I feel better about myself. I feel . . . here is a place where I'm respected and needed. Money isn't everything. We're all much happier and none of them want me to work again.

"There isn't anything that I can think of right now that I could do that is so rewarding that I think I can put my children aside and they will keep. Because they're not going to keep. Michael is thirteen. In another four years or so he might be off at school. Those years go by quickly."

A woman doesn't have to feel she's actually contributing something vital to society, but she does need to feel a sense of friendship with her co-workers and a feeling of respect from her boss. When that's missing, many women return home to the friends and family who make them feel needed.

Women who have a difficult situation at home but a job that offers friendship, respect, and vitality rarely quit the job to solve problems at home. They try to solve the problems at home first and quit their jobs only as a last resort. I met one woman who had quit because her husband objected to the way it was taking her away from their home. Two years later the couple was divorced and she was back to work. Lee, on the other hand, is still happily married, though not working.

Making work more pleasant and rewarding is the cheapest way employers can get better work from happier, more loyal employees. A company can let mothers bring their children in for visits, establish flexible work schedules, with allowances for childhood sickness and the like, create an atmosphere that is personal and productive without spending great quantities of money. Women used to being their own boss in a household will respond enthusiastically to working patterns that help them achieve pride in their domain and togetherness in their relations with others. Lee told me, for example, that the store's management had never allowed the women workers to organize their department or their relationships. But she felt they might have taken pride in its attractiveness (drapery material) and its total sales records if they had been allowed some management of their small alcove.

Many working mothers have a choice—they don't have to work all the time. Many work just to get over a difficult financial period —raising tuition for a child's college education or living through a recession. The fact that they have this choice means that they are more apt to quit a job that is demeaning. Many women, moreover, find they have more difficulties settling problems at home if they're dissatisfied with their jobs.

Coping problems fall roughly into two categories: the practical, everyday logistics of running a household and performing at work, and psychological stress, brought on by the pull of conflicting interests and social expectations. Most working mothers seem quite able, on the whole, to manage logistical problems. Many are superb managers, capable of coping with complex schedules and the thousand details of family life. When they flounder, it is usually because they are overwhelmed by psychological demands, the competing expectations of teachers, doctors, neighbors, friends, colleagues, and sometimes husbands insisting they are doing things the wrong way. They have their limits.

ten

ARE WORKING MOTHERS
SEXIER?

Impotence is on the rise, yes. Here at Harvard we have had a remarkable increase in impotency cases since the onslaught of women's liberation. These young men come in to complain of a condition that scares them. Their young women are slamming their fists down on the table and saying, "Satisfy me!" and the male reaction is panic. If their women can't have an orgasm, they feel failures. Some men, however, freeze up before they ever find out if their partners can have an orgasm. Both sides have lost any sense of leisure and relaxation in their sexual lives. A HARVARD PSYCHOLOGIST

Janis was thirty-nine, attractive in a full-blown, faintly overpowering way. She has two children, a good job, and some lively ideas about her sex life.

"The maturing of my sexuality was very much related to my work and to my experiences with other men. I experienced full orgasm and confidence in my sexuality with other men before I did with my husband. That wouldn't have happened if I'd been home all the time taking care of the children. Because before I went to work I didn't enjoy sex. And that became translated into 'You don't love me.' The reason I didn't enjoy sex was that I didn't come to orgasm. I felt something was wrong with me. That I was frigid. His readiness, and his two-minute orgasms began to mean 'He obviously desires and loves me more than I love him.'

"Instead of recognizing that his anxiety was related to his

premature ejaculation, I put it all on myself. And I couldn't win, because if I didn't have an orgasm, and wasn't satisfied, and was honest with him, he felt so horrible, so inadequate, and so depressed that that was my fault too. So I did a lot of faking. Which was frustrating and angered me, and it wasn't fair to him. But that seems to be the game women have to play.

"So I guess you can say that if I hadn't gone to work, I never would have had affairs with other men. My husband and I have been married now for nineteen years. I probably would still be faking it if it hadn't been for my career."

Many women report marital problems as a consequence of leaving home to "go out into the world of men." With or without affairs, many women feel their sex lives have changed. Many husbands, therefore, find that though they have a faithful wife, they still face sexual change in their marriage. Most women do not fully act out the changes in their sexuality, as Janis did, but her words hold general meaning for almost everyone I met in connection with this book.

"I think that my experience with other people both at my job and the friendships and sexual relationships I had were very important in terms of my having an identity that began to be separate from Arthur. One of the big difficulties that I had, and I think any woman has, was this: when you enter a marriage, you sense very quickly that the man's identity is much stronger, and Arthur had a very strong identity, even a public identity, so that I was always Arthur's wife, and it was very difficult for me to separate myself out from that. My work and my relationships were crucial in giving me times away from Arthur where I could pull myself back and people could react to me just as me. Work experience in that sense is truly one of the only ways in which you can have adult relationships that are not all tied in with your life at home."

Getting a new or stronger identity through adult relationships away from home apparently is one of the most intoxicating sidelights of the work experience. Especially for women returning to work, this identity surge has ramifications in many aspects of their lives, not the least of which is their sex lives and the possibility of experiencing sexual feelings that for many have been buried in the routine of housewifery.

Does this mean that working mothers are promiscuous? Less

than 5 per cent of the women I talked with admitted to having had extramarital affairs. Most "handled the situation of other men" through various means that tended to discourage sexual liaisons at the office.

"The first year I worked after our marriage I found that I was spending more time with a colleague, a man, than I was with my husband," one Connecticut woman told me.

"I realized right away that there were certain vibrations going around with this other guy. He was single and two years younger than I. I found him attractive and we worked well together so in a double sense we had this extra bond that I could never have with my husband—I mean my husband is an engineer and I am a clinical therapist. Our work has nothing in common. So finding this man whom I saw every day and worked with so closely—we are 'co-therapists'—was a threat to my husband even before I was aware of these vibrations.

"I could see this the first time I invited my colleague home for a social evening. My husband was very odd, and he didn't feel comfortable at all.

"So after a while I knew I had something I had better face up to. I was very young then in two ways—I was only twenty-six and I was very inexperienced. We had been married only two years and hadn't had the baby yet. I didn't talk to my husband about it at all. We simply avoided discussing the possibility that something might develop between this other guy and me. That made the tension even greater. I would go off to work feeling I was being covert or something. Then the little nuances began to multiply. You know the kind of thing I mean—lunches when our conversation would become personal and rather groping. Long deep looks into each other's eyes—every signal was out. Well, one day I found the tension intolerable and decided to take the bull by the horns and bring it out into the open—with him, not my husband.

"It was a Friday and I had spent the whole week privately thinking, What do I want anyway? Do I want to mess this all up? I had decided that I didn't want to, so I thought the best thing would be to confront him with my feelings. So I did it. I told him, 'Look, there's a lot going on between you and me and I want to talk about it.' I told him that I wanted to continue to work with him but that I couldn't if we didn't clear the air, that I felt these vibrations, that I thought he did too, but that I had decided

I didn't want to do anything about it and knew that unless we understood that, things were going to be unbearable.

"It turned out to have been a good thing. Once we discussed our feelings, we could acknowledge our good feelings for each other without all that sexual tension. We simply declared to each other that sex was not going to be a part of our relationship, and having made that decision, it was easier to become 'friends.' If we had a really good day, a warm moment, or shared something special in our work, it was easy, after our discussion, to exchange a friendly hug or some sort of open acknowledgment of our pleasure without any sexual tension.

"That was six years ago. Now, a mother and a wife and still working with men all the time, I find that that lesson has worked for me in other situations. I mean whenever I get these sexual vibrations from another man, whether or not I share them, I start right out by confronting them with a discussion. Just recently this happened with a young guy who had just come to work at our clinic, a place where, just by the nature of our work, feelings hang out all over the place. I didn't wait a week. The first chance I got to talk with him about it I did. Once again I told him that I felt these feelings with him, that I liked him very much, but that I had long ago decided that I wanted to keep my sexual life with my husband and didn't want to get messed up with anything outside that. I told him that I brought it up not because I wanted to embarrass either one of us but because I did like him so much and wanted to work with him without any misunderstandings.

"So that's the way I've learned to handle these matters and it has worked, for me anyhow. But there's another thing that I don't discuss with these men and that is what it all means in my marriage. A marriage, which is not always a honeymoon to say the least. First of all, I don't mean to imply that I go around getting turned on to some man at the clinic every week. These things happen rarely. But when they do occur, I have learned, and this comes right out of my own profession, to ask myself why. I mean what is it in this guy whoever he may be that is turning me on? What is he offering me that I'm not getting at home? I try to put my finger on what I think is attracting me. Usually I discover that there is something I need emotionally that I'm not getting from my husband at the time. If I can pinpoint it, I then talk to my husband about it and we can work on that. So in that sense, these little attractions, which really are more than little attractions because they're not just physical things, have served me well in my marriage. Not that I can get or expect to get everything I want or need from my husband, but I have been able so far to keep things pretty open and, at least, to divert my neediness from seeking sexual alliances with men who may seem to be able to compensate for what I don't get in my husband."

This woman held a Ph.D. in psychology and had a lot of experience in group therapy. Her solution to the problem of "other men" was clearly tied to her professional approach to human behavior. Many women who might find her experience attractive on paper have not developed an easy style that would lend itself to such open and forthright discussions. Yet nipping a relationship in the bud in some way or other seems to be a tactic that many women adopt.

"I invite the men whom I work closely with home to meet my family right away," a forty-six-year-old government administrator said. "I found this was the best way to waylay any fears my husband might have about the men I worked with and also that by seeing me in my home setting, with the kids and my husband, the men get a different picture of me than they do at the office. If they're married, I invite their wives too. That way, everybody gets the picture."

Many women, however, don't want to mix their social and professional lives or find that it is not appropriate for one reason or another. As one woman, a nurse, put it:

"I work in the operating room with a crew of male doctors. Our relationship, though intimate in many ways, is not the kind that makes me feel comfortable asking them home for dinner. Nurses just don't have the same status. Yet, as we scrub up and often gab with each other, the situation is full of opportunities for a pass and doctors are notorious for that. M*A*S*H was real in lots of ways. This hospital, full of beds you know, is full of a lot of hanky-panky. But I decided long ago not to do it. I've been known to flirt around a bit sometimes but I always keep it at a level that is understood to be all in fun. My husband and I joke about it. I tell him stories about things that go on here and we have nicknames for lecherous doctors. I tell him what 'hot pants' or 'the knife' are up to when I see them make a score and gradually I guess I've just acquired the reputation of being one of the guys."

Women who act to avoid problems before they develop do so primarily because they have made conscious, thought-through decisions about their own marriages. For whatever reason, they decide to maintain a monogamous marriage and choose whatever method they find comfortable to implement that decision. It doesn't necessarily mean their marriages are always smooth-running or satisfying. But their decision reflects a commitment to the marriage nevertheless.

Others look at their careers and decide they do not want to complicate their jobs with sex. These women, often struggling with a precarious marriage at home, see their jobs as another battlefront. They feel "representative" of women in their positions. To lie down, quite literally, with a man on the job, means they might be accused of being "typically feminine" at the office and not "professional."

These women, often faced with a relationship that looks like a blissful relaxation of a hundred tensions derived from their two treadmills, agonize much more about the decision to pass it by.

They don't expect such a situation to arise. They have been so busy at home and have had so much difficulty arranging for their careers that they hardly have the time to consider what getting out of the house might drag up in the way of further complications. Once out in the field, so to speak, they discover that both male and female relationships are available to them that they have not been exposed to since marriage.

The first time women realize they can explore a world alone and unvisited by their families, that they can become, in some fashion, the persons they were before marriage, is an intoxicating moment. Many change, both consciously and unconsciously, as they discover they can work at something previously considered gone out of their lives.

Getting out of that groove is pure excitement to many women. They find themselves with a new public image—an interesting conglomerate of hearth mother, serious worker, and experienced sybarite. Physically, they have matured. They may no longer exude a model's Yves St. Laurent image. But their broadened hips, often-nursed breasts, and stretched tummies have a message that isn't difficult to pick up. Place these women in the desk next to the man who married the girl next door, who is still home in the house that is similar to that other house which was similar to the house next door, and they pose a problem.

Turned on to a rejuvenation of dreams long buried, women returning to work are nakedly exposed to new stimuli. Unwittingly, some arrive at this new setting with barely concealed signs of marital strife, because getting to a rebirth of long-forgotten goals never happens overnight. It may start with a seed sown on an April morning, yet not achieve fruition until an Indian summer, six months later. I've never met a woman who decided on Tuesday to go back to work and found that by Wednesday everyone in her family agreed she had come up with a great idea.

Most women find they have struggled to maintain a status quo at home while subtly altering all the conditions that went into establishing that status quo. No one needs a Ph.D. in sociology to see that that is going to create tensions between a husband and wife.

Which is one way of saying that women often go off to work angry at their husbands, angry at the world, and absolutely determined, nevertheless, to swallow their anger and be terrific working mothers. So, fired up, they plunge themselves into their jobs, exhaust themselves with maintaining a household just as they always had (even if it's dirtier), and find that their marriages, which they have already "tampered with," begin to seem—temporarily at least—a painful reminder of what they have left behind.

So along comes a man from the office who sees this sensual, tense (mother) figure who is engaging, intelligent, hard-working, knowledgeable about matters which he has long since decided his own wife could care less about, and the game begins.

Except that there is no stereotyping of a real person's life. What happens to any single woman (or man) has to be dealt with by them, not by a book about people like them or by people trained to deal with those problems. So the agony goes on, isolated and personal, while at the same time it is plucked out of the human condition for the scripts of endless soap operas and comic strips.

One such woman, Penny, told me she felt very vulnerable to attacks from various segments of society—the media, women who were anxious to say "I told you so," men who had wives who

weren't in her position, mothers-in-law, or grandmothers. Penny
was thirty-five years old. She had been married for thirteen years.
She had two children, adorable sun-kissed boys (six and eight)
who tugged at her soft spots daily. Her husband was a doctor and
she had worked as a high school teacher through most of his training. Then she had gone back to graduate school in search of a
Ph.D. She was a full-time student, which meant she had more
than an eight-hour day, every day. Evenings were work times, day
times were work times. Her kids and her husband were sand-
wiched in between hours that she could take off from her studies.

Penny was a complicated person with or without graduate
school. She had graduated from Bryn Mawr, a Phi Beta Kappa in
her junior year. Brought up in Wichita, Kansas, she had long
regarded herself as the black sheep of an otherwise simple and
"God-fearing" family. She had a great aunt who was a missionary
in China and everyone in her family told her that was the source
of her genetic discontent. But she had tried. She married right out
of college and everyone applauded the union. When she had her
first child, she arranged her time to his schedule and no one con-
demned her "work" because she was, after all, helping to meet expenses while her husband went through the military. She fit into a
wifely role that her husband's colleagues saw as commendable.
Rush-rush though it was, it was nevertheless par for the course.

Penny's problems started with her husband's final year of
residency. Their finances were no longer a pressing problem. He
worked at extra jobs and earned $20,000 a year and they were
prepared to buy their first house and look forward to more lucra-
tive years just around the corner. Penny had found superb child
care for her sons, who got home at 2:30 every afternoon. Her husband, tired of all the stress his training had produced through
most of the years of their marriage, wanted to unwind a bit. He
wanted to go places on weekends with the kids, have a few drinks
and watch television at night, spend more money than they had
allowed themselves before. The last thing he wanted was a woman
offering him a bundle of nerves, constant fatigue from overwork,
and a new set of anxieties. Which is what he ended up with.

Penny explained what had happened:

"This last year, as I saw Ron relax a bit, I think I unconsciously
let myself go with all the things I had bottled up while he was
working so hard. Whatever my reasons, I found that I increasingly

felt unhinged. My work this year is very taxing. I have to be at the University until 7 P.M. on three days. That means I don't really see the boys at all, except for breakfast and bedtime. During breakfast we're all rushing and I feel awful because I am so tired. At bedtime I'm done in physically and emotionally too. So I've got a lot of guilt about this but it's the only way I can get through the program.

"So given this state of fatigue and pressure I haven't got very much back from Ron all year. I mean, he simply hasn't had a lot of patience or something because I have got to the point where I hide all my painful feelings because I know that he will only be irritated by them. We've had a rough year. I would say it's the closest we've ever come to splitting up. There have been a couple of really big fights that have been landmarks for us and I don't see it as getting any easier."

Not "getting much" at home left Penny wide open to a relationship at work which seemed to offer her all the nurturing she was longing for. As part of a fellowship she worked with an assistant professor in a related department. He was her age, married, and childless. His wife worked as a secretary part time and they were a bit on edge as she had been trying to get pregnant for three years. So he seemed ripe for some affirmation of his own maleness. Their relationship grew from a platonic, respectful friendship to a personal, intimate, warm need for each other. They had not gone to bed with each other, although they discussed their desire to. Both agreed that they didn't want to give up on their marriages, but as the year went on, both realized that their marriages were in trouble anyhow.

"There were so many opportunities for Michael and me to have an affair all that spring that it seems foolish we didn't. Then came the crunch. We were offered a large grant to work on a project that would take at least three years and would mean a lot, especially to my own career. Not only would I be earning money before I had even finished my thesis, but I could use the work for a thesis. It was the perfect setup. But we both knew if we were going to be working that closely with each other, our feelings for each other would inevitably explode.

"I decided not to take it. I made the decision alone, without consulting either Michael or Ron. This is the way I put it to myself. My marriage is miserable right now, but it wasn't before, and it may not always be so. My relationship with Michael is strained because of unconsummated sexual tension, so we're always too happy to see each other, if you know what I mean. The only thing that is really solid and right for me right now is my work, which I have kept at throughout all the personal turmoil and which I have more confidence in than anything else in my life —except maybe for my children, who somehow do fit into the picture too although not in this particular structure I seem to be creating for you.

"The point is that I agonized over what to do for a few days and decided that I was crazy to take the grant with Michael. Not, mind you, because I am afraid what it would do to my marriage. That marriage is going to have to face up to things pretty soon anyway and it may split up even if I have nothing to do with another man for the rest of my life.

"I could see that if I continued on with my dance with Michael, it would work itself into my work eventually. I didn't want to mess with my career is what it all boils down to. I did see myself as responsible for any reputation I might acquire if it got out that I slept with my lab partner. But I wasn't worried about what went on behind my back so much as I was about the direction I would be going in if I mixed what was serious and rewarding work with personal, sexual relationships.

"I admit that I thought of the kids and my marriage and all that I had invested in that, but working mothers lead a number of lives and their careers are like one of them. I think sometimes you have to isolate them all to see them clearly and make decisions about them that are relatively objective."

Penny's story is unfinished. For all I know she is now working with someone else while maintaining an affair with Michael and dealing periodically with her marital problems. But her decision to keep her professional dealings clean interested me. Many women who seem to have some trouble dealing with the complexities of their family relations hasten to place their careers on self-protected pedestals.

For some it is simply good politics. If a woman works in a small office where everyone knows exactly what everyone else is doing or senses what everyone else is doing, a woman is not going to open herself up to gossip. At least this seems to be true for working mothers.

But some women feel they are only out of the kitchen by the grace of God, and they'll go right back to the P.T.A. presidency if they mess up in any way. The easiest way to lose this God-given opportunity is to have an affair with someone at work. If they are going to have an affair, they would choose someone completely unrelated to their careers, but as one woman put it, "When am I going to have *time* to conduct an affair with someone who isn't living either in my house or at my office?"

Some women who have no plans for sexual relations with a colleague develop friendships at work that are difficult for their families to swallow. By "families," I mean primarily their husbands. Children rarely care much about the intensity of any involvement their mothers may have with other adults—as long as they don't make the mistake of spending too much time elsewhere. But some husbands have difficulty dealing with their wives' professional relationships, especially if the woman's work is in a field that offers no social backdrop for them to comfortably join in on together. One woman, for example, a day-care teacher, had developed a number of friendships with young men who also taught at the center. Her husband is a lawyer whose professional life is worlds away from the blue jeans and tie-dyed world of the day-care center. He found himself feeling stiff around the people his wife works with and he didn't like the way these other guys would give his wife a hug in the morning as he let her off at the center.

"My husband just doesn't understand these guys. They are earning about $60 a week and he's earning more than $600 a week so they are worlds apart in the way they live and in the way they choose to spend their time. He can't understand why they'd want to spend their 'most productive' years earning next to nothing and playing with kids. And when he sees me enjoying them so much, he thinks, If she can enjoy them so much, maybe she doesn't enjoy me so much, or something like that. He is very obviously threatened by them and piqued by my attentions to them. Our children are too old for day-care centers and we never had them when they were little. So he doesn't know from firsthand experience how personal such a place is and how much these feelings are necessary for a homey atmosphere."

This woman learned to protect her husband. She kept her relationships at work deliberately separate and quiet. She led two lives, quite literally. Her at-home entertainment consisted of dinner parties that included her husband's colleagues but never her own. The only way in which she tried to include her family in her professional life was with her children, who, aged nine, eleven, and fifteen, liked to come to the center sometimes to help out. They "dug it."

In spite of the fact that few working mothers become involved with "other men," the spectre of such men affects them. For most the affects are good ones.

"Getting out of the house every single day has been terrific for me. I have lost some weight, I dress with more care, and people tell me I look younger," a Cambridge secretary explained. "When I was home in the suburbs every day, I would eat and cook to pass the time. It was like I was stuffing things in me to compensate for the lack of things going on around me. At thirty I found that I was matronly. That shook me up a bit and so I got this job, which my husband, a lawyer, felt was fine, if that was what I wanted. Now I'm much more aware of my role in an adult world that I want to be included in, recognized in. I think my physical appearance is probably indicative of the changes that have gone on inside me as I awakened to the fact that life was not over yet. No need to be a matron at thirty."

"Working has heightened my sense of sexuality," another woman said. She had been at home for five years with two small children. Now she worked full time as a political aid to a congressman. Her youngest, age two, was in a day-care center she had helped to organize. "I loved my years at home with the babies but they were very maternal most of the time. Now I find that it is very exciting to be out in the world, so to speak, and still have this other private, maternal part of me too. I feel very womanly, being a working mother—it's so much that I have got both things I think. I've fulfilled two dreams and every day is rather nice proof of it. I'm more turned on to myself and everyone else.

"When I've had a good day of work I've noticed that I feel sexier. There is that rush of pleasure at having got something good done and having instigated it. It leaves me more full of life than housework or constant child care. Even if I'm tired, I'm less tired —I mean I get a second wind and I look forward to my evenings with the family. On those nights I am often the initiator of sex. I zip around doing the things I have to and whenever I get the chance I go give my husband a nibble on the ear or something. I am happy and rather proud of myself, which of course rubs off in my relations with my husband." This woman is a writer and part-time high school teacher.

Feeling sexier, feeling more turned on, thinner, prettier, or less matronly is an important, fundamental reaction. Whether it comes from "being out of the house" or exposure to other men makes little difference. Working mothers who exhibit a heightened sense of sexuality find that it is noticeable to other people as well as to themselves. That means husbands notice too, and different husbands react to this phenomenon in different ways.

Some, fortunately, think it's just great. Others, unfortunately, find their working wives' sexuality disturbing. They are unsettled by a change that manages to suggest, subtly, that they've got to work a bit harder to keep and satisfy a newly revived wife. An old college professor of mine, Andrew Hacker, sent me an article he had written some years ago on the husbands of working wives. A "Husband of a Working Wife" himself, he had this to say:

> . . . It is up to the HWW to ensure that his wife's affections remain in one place. Put another way, the HWW has more *potential* competitors and he is therefore obliged to work harder at making his marriage durable and successful. It certainly means that the HWW cannot take his wife for granted, nor can he afford bouts of irrational jealousy. No perceptive husband indulges himself in these luxuries anyway, but the HWW is even less in a position to forget the compliments and the affectionate understanding that men are apt to neglect. Certainly there is no prima-facie reason to be jealous of the men in one's wife's work-life. . . .
>
> There is a theory, [he goes on,] that a riskier game is all the more worth playing because of the greater satisfactions accruing to those who can carry it off successfully. . . . But the final word must be that the well-advised HWW will avoid all sexual suspicions and recriminations. For a show of unfounded jealousy may well turn fantasy into cruel fact.

Men who don't come naturally to this conclusion have sometimes paid a fearful price for their failure of perception. Although I found few women who admitted that their husbands' suspicions, jealousy, or neglect had driven them into someone else's bed, many women talked of the alienation in their marriage that stemmed from their husbands' inability to accept the vibrancy, sexual or otherwise, that arose naturally out of their work experience.

I can't pretend that I understand male psychology well enough to explain this apparently widespread male insecurity. But many working mothers clearly live with men who cannot see their wives' growth and enjoyment of life outside the confines of their homes as anything but a threat to the happiness of the "household," the "family," the "children," or themselves.

These jealous feelings pose particular problems for working mothers. Women *without* children, married to men who are unreasonably suspicious of them or threatened by them, might well not put up with it. But working mothers have a hard time dealing squarely with the problem—and not because they are convinced that they ought to hold the marriage together "for the children's sake." Working mothers, perhaps uniquely, tend to share a feeling, a deeply buried fear, that their husbands, *perhaps all men*, are close to an essential truth. Perhaps their private delight at being a productive worker *is* selfish; maybe they *ought* to be viewed with apprehension. Possibly they *should* feel some guilt about this "best of both worlds" life that they thrive on. One woman said to me, "How can I expect my husband not to feel threatened, when I know that I *am* a threat—we [working mothers] are a threat to a whole tradition of family harmony, male supremacy, and domestic management. I can't tell him it's a figment of his imagination. It's not. I feel strong, successful, independent, and sensual. And I work with a lot of men every day, five days a week. That has to be a turn-on, even if nothing comes of it."

Women may feel they ought to be satisfied baking bread and rearing babies, and once they discover they can really handle more —the babies, the bread, *and a job*—they feel enlightened, suddenly liberated, and quite possibly superior. Furthermore, they enjoy their motherhood status, their maternal feelings and performance as proof of their femininity. So, feminine and competent (in a professional world previously dominated by males), they feel stronger than their husbands (particularly if their husbands find this duality hard to accept). Women who don't feel superior usually have husbands who have no difficulty taking over some of the traditional feminine roles—that of housekeeper and child-rearer. A husband who can do both things—because they are there—without feeling debased, emasculated, or shaken in his view of life's domestic arrangements is unlikely to feel threatened by his wife's newfound joy of competence. She is, after all, doing no more than *he's* been doing all along, and often (let us admit it) with less professional expertise.

In short, the simplest way for a husband to remove all cause for potential anxiety may be to establish a genuine parity in relationships between man and wife, husband and father. Once men become "accustomed" to women, as functional equals rather than biological curiosities, they find it easier to understand why women are susceptible to the same temptations—as well as the same restraints—known to working men for generations.

How do women feel about suspicious or threatened husbands? Whenever I asked a woman why she stayed with a husband who continually made her feel bad, or guilty, she answered, "Because I pity him."

This seems to be especially true of women struggling financially to stay alive. The poorer a family, the less likely it is that either husband or wife will consider divorce a viable emotional alternative. They seem in a double bind. Studies show that women who work, but would prefer not to, report a less satisfactory marital adjustment, an increase in marital tensions for husbands, and a decrease in marital satisfaction for wives. If a husband strongly disapproves of his wife's employment status, marital adjustment is likely to be significantly less congenial.*

One woman who worked as a clerk in a hardware store told how her eighteen years of marriage had been marred by her husband's insistence that, after two years of marriage, she give up a well-paid secretarial job to stay home with her baby. A few years later she had been forced to get a lower paying job because they needed the money.

"My husband didn't like my working. I was making the same pay that he was. He was working sixty hours and I was working thirty-seven and a half and he didn't like it at all. I had to work though because I had no insurance when I had the baby and we had all kinds of bills. We had been married less than a year.

"It was the male ego I guess you'd call it, and people used to make remarks. 'I'd never let my wife work. She should be home

* S. R. Orden and N. M. Bradburn, "Working Wives and Marriage Happiness," *American Journal of Sociology*, Vol. 74, No. 397, 1969.

with the baby.' That kind of thing. I don't know if he thought I should be home with the baby, I think it was more the money. When I look back, I wish common sense had told us. . . . He's a very handy person, he likes making things. I was making the same pay and working less. He should have stayed home and I should have worked. I would have been making twice the pay he's making now. And in a job that I liked. That was fifteen years ago, and now I would have been eligible for a pension. Your insurance was all paid, life and health. I really had a good job, but because of this screwed-up society I had to give it up and I think, to this day, I'm still resentful of it.

"When I had to quit that job, I wasn't lonely, 'cause I had a lot of friends. But I was bored. I'm not the house type. Although I tried. I was very young. I was only twenty and very inhibited sexually—Catholic upbringing, Catholic schools—so I had very little release for anything when I was at home. My job offered me some of that. But my husband would get very jealous because of the men there.

"To be honest with you, I think I've outgrown him. He escapes, where I'll face something. He'll escape it. In different ways . . . in his work, or he'll come home with a six pack of beer, to relax himself when he is bothered. Where I won't. I'll face it and it would be much easier if the two of us faced it. When you face things alone, you grow up in a hard sense. You get bitter. I know it shows but I can't help it.

"But I don't think it's an individual's fault. Like I can't really blame my husband, because he was brought up to think this way. I think we (women) have to change that, we really do, in the way we raise our children.

"Now I don't like my job so much. I feel I'm worth much more. I used to get $2.50 and now I get $2.75 an hour and some of that is under the table but I feel that for the work that I do . . . like it sounds very simple, waiting on customers, but it doesn't stop there. It's a very physical job and a very mental job. When I'm there, I'm one of these that puts my whole heart and soul into it. There's a lot of ways things that you could do would be very costly to the owner and it happens constantly with everyone else that's working for him. I can honestly say that it's never happened with me. And I feel he knows this and I feel I should get at least $3.50 without a question. So when I asked him, I got the quarter; and I told him, 'You must have been up all night writing the little note' he wrote me when I got the quarter.

"I think working as a secretary changed my feelings about myself. I think working makes me feel independent which I'm the type that has to be that way. I think he, my husband, would like it the other way. But it's my nature, what can you do? I've thought of leaving him. But what stops me? . . . Pity. I would never stay with him for the kids' sake because that's an excuse, that doesn't work. In a sense I'm wrong by staying with him. But I'm afraid of the guilt I would have if I left him. I'm worried about that. It's me I'm worried about because I'm doing him as much harm here as I would if I'd thrown him out on the streets. I know this. Instead of throwing him out to make him grow up, I don't. It's like you protect your kids and yet I say you shouldn't and yet I do it, right? . . . with him. That's why I say you know what's right, but it's another thing doing it."

I found many working-class women who stayed with their husbands for the same reason. Middle-class women tended not to acknowledge that position. Maybe they shared it, but they were careful not to bring it out into the open. I did find middle-class women who divorced husbands who'd become threatened by their wives' careers, jealous of their wives' time out of the house and the possibility of relationships with other men, and worried about the new set of expectations their wives seemed to thrust at them.

One woman, a television executive, had been married for seventeen years. She had worked for the first five years, then took eight years out to care for three children. For the past four years, however, she had been working full time, and through a combination of her own abilities and one very fortunate retirement in the company had been promoted to an important high-level management position. She was in love with her work. It was, of course, a drastic change in her life.

Kate came from a small New England town. She had never lost her country Yankee accent, which was now a source of some amusement in her sophisticated office. Nor had she lost any of the traditional feelings she had been brought up with on the duties of a mother.

"My own mother was home and happy all the time I was growing up. She was an important source of love and peace for me and I try to give my own three daughters the same feeling. Which means I devote every free moment I have to my family. Not with any resentment. I love them and really enjoy them. They're great kids, pretty, loving, and fun. In many ways it's like having three little sisters. We are very close.

"But what went on between my husband and me is tied up to that. He wanted to be nurtured by me too . . . the way children do. He literally wanted me to have five clean hankies ironed in his top drawer every night. I felt like he wanted me to be his mother and see that his wardrobe and lunch box were ready for school each day.

"When I first went back to work, we had a lot of arguments over those kinds of things. He wanted everything to remain the same and of course it couldn't. I simply wasn't able to nurture him all the time. I couldn't cook as much. I couldn't be on top of all the housework all the time. I couldn't regard our weekends the same way as we used to—which is to say that I used to see them as a time for him to relax because he had been working so hard all week. Afterwards, I saw them as a time for both of us to pitch in to take care of all the things that didn't get taken care of during the week so that we could have some fun together before Monday morning came along. I resented taking the girls out of the house all Saturday afternoon and all Sunday afternoon while he watched football games because I was dead tired after two days of walking through museums, parks, zoos, or playgrounds.

"So, you see, I thought I had a simple battle of 'pigginess' in my own home and was treating my problems then as if what I had to do was make him see the 'feminists' line.' But things got worse and eventually, after about eighteen months of squabbling, we went to a marriage counselor.

"To make a long story short, it turned out in therapy that Bill was not so worried about who did the housework and all the logistical problems at home as he was using these battles to get the message in my head that he wanted me to quit working and go home because he felt threatened by my working—by the men in my office, by my new figure (I lost fifteen pounds in the first year of work), by the aggressive way I seemed to take on the world in every aspect of my life—like the way I talked at parties, the way I had gained status in our social circles—by the suspicion he seemed to have that I would find some other man.

"Even after we got all these feelings out on the table, that didn't make them all go away. We simply moved into a new phase of our troubles. Bill tried doing more around the house, he tried being with the girls more, he really tried on all the battlefronts we had but he couldn't conceal his concern and his suspicions seemed to fester in him even more. For a while he was impotent.

"We went back to the marriage counselor. I had been working for two and a half years and I had just gotten my big promotion. By this time, it is true that I had changed. I was much more self-confident—both in my work and in my mothering. Bill didn't want this new Kate. He wanted the old one back and although we gave our marriage another year of intense therapy, and a real try to work out our problems, it was no good. Bill was depressed a lot, his work suffered, and finally, after this last summer when we took a long vacation together on a lake with the kids and an attempt to give it one last push, we both decided to separate.

"Now here's the funny thing about our separation, which I should add is most certain to go into divorce soon. Everybody who knows us says to me, 'Admit it, Kate, it was *the job* wasn't it? If it hadn't been for *the job*, your marriage would have stayed together.' I say no, in *this* sense. It wasn't the job so much, you see, as it was the image of myself that evolved from my career. You see, I had come to expect more from a relationship. Bill's childlike worry about my working, the kind you can imagine a four-year-old would have when he saw his mother going back to work—that he was going to lose her, that she was going to people and places that he didn't know about and would care more for them than for him whenever she went off to work in the morning. That was a big turn-off. I found it difficult to relate to him as a man, after a few years of that. His moodiness if I had to have a meeting in the evening with a bunch of male colleagues was similar to a two-year-old's temper tantrums. I got so that I felt that I couldn't tell him about my luncheon engagements whenever they weren't with women. If I bought clothes that were alluring and sexy, he expressed distaste for them. Or he would tell me I was spending too much money on clothes—that, in face of the fact that we were making more money than we could ever possibly spend. I stopped wearing a bra and he had a fit. He would drop into the office and be surly with my colleagues.

"So you see, I needed more from a relationship; I needed a man

who would be turned on *himself* by the excitement I felt inside
me and not be threatened by it. I began to feel sorry for him, and
how can you be married to a man whom you pity?"

Kate's story is a common divorce story among those working
mothers I talked with who are now single. As another woman put
it, "It wasn't the long hours of my work that bothered my husband. It was my enthusiasm." Kelly had worked all of her married
life. Her ambitions were never troublesome to her husband until
she had her first child.

"I was married when I was nineteen and I had just graduated
from college. I got a really top job in a firm that I always wanted
to work in. I didn't have children for six years and I worked full
time the whole time. My husband and I were both very ambitious, he and I would leave at 7:45 in the morning and go to a
coffee shop for breakfast, and literally I'd be at the office by 8:15
and stay there until 6:30. I worked hard all the time. I brought
work home on weekends and I sort of slept and ate and breathed
it. I loved it, I really loved it. There was really no other way to
live. We lived in a dark apartment and had no money and what
do you do, you work. So it was fun, it was part of my growing,
because I was so young when I was married. It was part of my
identity.

"When my first child was born, I had become a senior executive with my own department in the firm. I worked the day she
was born, went to the hospital and nursed her. I remember taking
phone calls and no one was at all aware that I had just become a
mother. I took two weeks off to have my baby but I was still on
the phone a lot and I kept time sheets. Then I started to go back
to the office. And because my work is really a produce-or-get-lost
situation, I really did have to go back. I'd come home and nurse
the baby and then go back. I only nursed for three months with
each child and I lived a few blocks from my office. I never let the
office know that I was nursing.

"What was happening to me during this period was that,
through my success and through these new womanly feelings I
had after I became a mother, I was gaining confidence in myself
that made me feel I could tackle anything, do anything, go anywhere. I was shedding all my fears.

"That was when we started having marital troubles. My husband's family was very traditional. None of the women ever

worked. They were smart women, well educated, and nonproductive. So they all assumed that now that I had a baby, I would quit. I laughed it off until my husband joined the chorus. My answer to him was to work harder at all the things in my life—I mean I'd rush home to make fantastic meals; I'd see that the housekeeper kept the house just beautifully clean and pretty; and I'd practically smother the babies with attention, always reading to them myself, taking lunches with them, spending all the weekend time with them. I was trying to say, 'See, I can do it. Don't worry.'

"But he did worry and he started trying to cut me down. He would criticize my work and we started to have impotency problems. I felt my problem was 99 per cent self-inflicted because I had to work, but if I didn't work, my problem would go away. But I loved my work so much that I couldn't do it from that vantage point.

"So, for the last few years of our marriage, we had a nonmarriage. There was a block and it was the most miserable thing to live with. I was talking with a friend one day, and we said that we probably have emotional orgasms in our work which compensate for lack of sex. But that's hardly a substitute, you know. With my husband, I would cry. I would have such longings I just wanted to touch him, to share it all, extend it. I never had an affair. I never had another flittering or anything for twelve years. He would claim that I had my period, or that I was going to get my period, or that I was in between my period and he would always blame our problem on my period. And I would cry. I got these desperate backaches. I just wanted him to massage me, to comfort me. I'd build up these tremendous enthusiasms, in my life, my world, my creativity. I wanted to have it released. He had blocked himself into thinking that he couldn't grow in that way too. Of course he could have. And he probably needed it just as much as I did. But he blocked himself into thinking that men just unzipped their flies four times a month or whatever. He didn't get into the real world of love, which is what it's all about.

"The longer his impotency lasted, the more he accused me of having flirted with someone, or having an attraction for someone at the office. And he would invite people over for dinner who were parents, but the wife didn't work. That was the final game he played. I love to give dinner parties and feel happy and glamorous as we enjoy this beautiful apartment and all the things we have here and just to share it with other people and enjoy them is a great source of pleasure for me. So he started inviting all these couples, I don't know where he got them, but sure enough, the wife stayed home with the kids. And I was made to feel so uncomfortable.

"I was lonely too. I didn't have anyone to identify with. I didn't know any other women who worked like I did, and were mothers. But not now. Since our separation and divorce, I've found lots of friends that I invite home. Now I don't have to worry about whether or not my husband will like them or be nice to them.

"One really hard thing I had to face was the accusation my husband made that I was a castrating woman. That's about the worst thing anyone can say to me. And here he was all limp to prove it. But I think he is wrong. I mean I don't think I'm mean or vicious or calculatingly out to get anyone. I never belittled him in public. Or private. It may seem that a man is castrated by his wife's talents, but it's not that at all. To say that assumes that a man has no say in the matter—like helpless, he stands by while his wife mows him down. That's not realistic. At least I feel that if men are castrated by working mothers, they've done the snipping themselves."

Kate and Kelly had extreme situations. Most husbands seem better able to cope with the changes in their wives since they had children or have taken on a job. Yet some men, even though they are not impotent, feel sexually threatened. But they are not threatened by an actual affair. Their wives are not seeking or accepting extramarital alliances. The threat is more subtle, more into the core, and more difficult to deal with.

Other men never feel threatened at all by wives who work. Some because they have learned to enjoy the same things in life their wives have—good work and a good job, pride and satisfaction in the management of a home, and an addiction to the rewards of being good parents. Some of these husbands iron their *own* handkerchiefs or fold them wrinkled. They know their way around supermarkets and around a kitchen stove. They recognize their kids' teachers on sight, know when the last tetanus shot has been given, and, when they go off on a trip with the family, never forget the Linus blanket for their youngest. These men, on the whole, are secure in their private and professional lives, and respectful of their wives' ambitions. Her achievements, wherever they occur, make her all the more attractive, vindicate his judgment in having spotted her in the first place, and give him cause for excitement, in bed and out of it, rather than fear, dread, rancor, and finally isolation.

Even so, the typical pattern is less hopeful. Whatever a woman's appeal, regular employment—along with the self-appraisal, increased confidence, and widening horizons that involves—seems to make her all the more attractive. What happens then, in logic, has less to do with her job, per se, than with the other circumstances of her life. And in this case, as in so many others, the true importance of the work situation is that it represents a change: it upsets a familiar equilibrium, giving both husband and wife a problem of adjustment.

Husbandly apprehensions (and it must occur to many of them that their wives have always accepted the reality of diverse human contact outside the home) must surely have a root in social conventions of a complex sort. Why, to put it bluntly, are husbands less trusting than wives? The answer, assuming good faith on both sides, surely has something to do with the homemaker model women have been living with for some four or five hundred years, and the way in which that model has shaped, simultaneously, a belief in male pre-eminence in the work force, and a confidence that as long as women are economically dependent they will also be sexually timid.

Mature males seem to come to terms with their sexual aggressiveness, but a quantum leap in imaginativeness is required, evidently, to persuade them that women can also harness their sexual ambitions, even while realizing their hopes for substantive accomplishment on their jobs.

Many women, like many men, will take advantage of the opportunities that present themselves, for roughly the same reasons.

The important point to make, in the face of these complicated issues, is that their complications transcend questions as simple as whether or not a *working* mother is, in any important way, likely to alter, or betray her marital assumptions. Women will be joining the work force in increasing numbers, and many of them will be mothers. That is a fact, not a debatable issue. What must be realized is how that will change their lives and therefore their families' lives. Honest intentions, recognition of mutual integrities, and ordinary self-respect are likely the best antidote to the problems that will surely follow.

eleven

HUSBANDS STEREOTYPED

I think the only time my husband has complained about my working has been when I've hurt myself or been sick and I'd get up in the morning feeling bad but getting ready to go to work. He'd say, "Why don't you stay home?" The guy I'm married to (I'd never tell him this) but he's really fantastic. He chips in when he comes home, even when he's tired. Even if I didn't love him, I don't think I'd get rid of him. Because I don't think there's another man like him really. He'll do anything—wash the dishes, vacuum, make the beds, wash a floor. One thing that happened recently was when we decided to remodel this kitchen, he said he was going to build the kitchen around the dishwasher and then he planned the whole kitchen so he could work better in it." A NURSE

I could not have spent over a year talking with working mothers, their husbands and children, without accumulating a set of impressions about their husbands. And I submit, with a trace of embarrassment, that these husbands seem to fall into four basic categories. I'd distrusted the patterns of "types" which I began to perceive, realizing the fallacy of making generalizations about people. But nevertheless, the same patterns continued to emerge, and so I include these general observations, partly in jest and partly because they may somehow be helpful.

Type A husbands, otherwise known as "professionals," are very informed on feminist issues. They are what might be called full-timers. They've studied the rules of the game, they know feminist rhetoric and are sensitive to its distinctions. They don't, for instance, "help out." They do "what needs to be done."

A "professional" takes his role as husband of a working wife seriously. It is, in fact, his second profession, and its demands are as important to him as the demands made on him at the office.

Professionals accept all the principles of an egalitarian marriage and work hard at becoming a psychological parent. They start with prenatal exercises and carry right through into high school. A professional may be the busiest doctor in town but if an eight-year-old has a dentist's appointment on Thursday afternoon and his wife is in conference, he'll pick up the child and get there. Type A's actively pursue the rearing of their children. Not just dentist's appointments, but teacher's conferences, bedtime conversations, and private trips to museums with individual siblings. Type A's know the ins and outs of all household appliances and schedules, and have a working knowledge of food preparation and shopping.

A Type A sees to it that his wife can pursue her own career just as he has pursued his. If, at some point, she made it possible for him to go to medical school, he, at some point, will kill himself to see that she can go to graduate school. Likewise, if she has had a few days of horrendous child-care and household responsibilities, he will take over as soon as possible and make sure that she gets a break. He has a perpetual measuring stick operating inside him to make sure that his wife is getting a fair shake.

A Type A may, however, be a striver. His marital pose may not come naturally to him. Maybe his mother didn't work, or if she did, his father made few concessions to her. His efforts, consequently, sometimes give him a certain edginess which suggests that he is being very careful not to be caught in a sexist blunder. He may, for instance, stumble frantically with soup plates into the kitchen—at someone else's house. Or interrupt party talk to point out that a *woman* has made a sexist remark. Men too. But deep in his heart he knows he gets two points for sniffing out the former, only one point for mentioning the latter.

A humorless pro can be a terrible drag. Carried to extremes, "deadpan determination" can be construed as condescending and boorish. The best Type A is liberated enough to tell his wife to get out of bed some morning at 6:30 so he can get some extra sleep.

Perhaps the greatest risk a Type A has to take is that he will become such a fine companion and living partner that he will cease to exist in the game of love. Many women who live without Type A's may resist the idea but the fact is that being equal parents, equal housekeepers, equal people, may equalize everything else. A Type A is especially susceptible to this problem because he works so hard to affirm his equality. He may be trying so hard, he gets a little nervous. His continual self-examination, his willingness to go on the stump for working mothers and therefore their marriages, can make him a bit evangelical. In spite of—or perhaps because of—Type A's determined efforts then, his wife discovers she has become something a good deal less than a sex object. She has become, instead, a proving ground for her own husband.

Feminist literature has at least one recurring theme, that men have consciously shifted the burden of domestic scutwork to women for at least several hundred years, and that it is about time to even things up. It's no wonder that a good many conscientious husbands drift apologetically into a position of acquiescence to this design, even if their earnestness goes far beyond the expectations or desires of their wives. All people want to be respected, and most women have a rough idea of the sort of equity to which they feel entitled. But few women (or men) want a spouse whose devotion to egalitarianism obscures his or her spontaneous sense of fun. Playing a more personal game may be more fruitful in the long run.

This may sound rather theoretical but it isn't. The divorce rate among "sensitive," "educated," "liberated" couples trying to bring up children while pursuing two careers is dismayingly high and on the increase. One woman I talked with, a history professor who hadn't had any children yet, told me, "My husband and I keep talking about having children someday, but I'm fearful of it. So many of my friends in academia who have tried holding onto their careers while taking care of young children have ended up divorced. And it wasn't a matter of a husband or wife being unwilling to go fifty-fifty. It's that the struggle was so hard, their marriage got dried up in the process."

Two ambitious, aggressive, talented, educated, liberalized people who want to live *equally, all the time*, seem to need a lot of unrehearsed flexibility. When a deadpan Type A perceives that, in spite of his perpetual effort, the scales start to tip so that he ends up taking on a larger share of the burden than his wife, he gets mad. Simple requests take on emotionally charged, political overtones. The elasticity of their relationship is stretched to the breaking point. Sooner or later, it will snap. And even if it doesn't snap, it's apt to shrivel. Marriage with a Type A can sometimes need the moistening that comes with lust, humor, and strong souls.

Type B: The Amateurs. Lambs dressed as lions, or is it the other way around? Either one will do. Type B's know little about feminist jargon, literature, or issues. When they hear about liberation they are likely to blush and say "That's a fine thing." What they mean is that women ought to be treated well.

Type B's married for love and never got over it. They still open the car door, or any other door for their wives, without thinking. It's not that they're crude lunks who don't have the wit to tune into the seventies and to the subtle battles that are going on in so many of their neighbor's homes. It's that they are basically satisfied with their marriages and have got what they had assumed they would get when they took the marital plunge. A Type B is most apt to have had a working mother, and to have absorbed, as routine, the peculiarities that follow.

B's pull most of their weight in the management of a household but the division of chores may be more traditionally oriented than in the home of a Type A. A Type B would willingly hire a maid or housekeeper if he could afford it. An A would not, of course, because he would not want to exploit anyone, least of all a woman. The greatest difference between the two when it comes to domestic responsibilities is that B's tend to do the heavy stuff like the yard, the exterior of the house, the garage, the upkeep of the car, the trash, maybe even the shopping and accounts; B's wife meanwhile does the cooking, laundry, lunch boxes, school clothes, pediatrician, P.T.A., and light housekeeping. In an A household those chores would be jumbled up so that everybody got a little light and little heavy work. A's don't "fall into" patterns at all. They "work things out."

When a B does the weekly grocery shopping, he hopes he got what his wife wanted, buys whatever is cheap or is known to be a family favorite. An A, on the other hand, is apt to read the unit pricing labels and win his spurs as a home economist.

B's are glad their wives are working. "I hope you write about the husbands of working wives," one B told me, as he caressed the back of his wife's neck in the living room of their split-level ranch in the middle of Indiana corn country. A color television set sat opposite the sofa and a gold shag wall-to-wall carpet covered the floor. "We're lucky. I wouldn't have her [slapping her thigh] any other way." Many B's made a point of telling me how important their wives' salaries were to the running of the household. Many wanted to make sure I knew that their wives had been promoted recently or that they had important jobs. One B came up to me at a party and said, "You ought to interview my wife for your book; she's been teaching for twenty-five years. She can tell you what it's like to be a working mother."

If an A wanted me to learn about his wife, he'd probably be much more subtle about it. An A would not want to be caught speaking for his wife, or making a display of her that would impinge on her right or ability to make her own way to the people she wants to meet. B's, on the other hand, tend to see themselves as part of a team. If a B meets someone he thinks would enjoy meeting his "teammate" he's likely to insist on the three of them getting together. An A would hesitate to impose on his wife's right to make her own conquests.

Most B's know a bit less about their children's development and progress than A's do. They rarely go with their daughters to buy clothes for school, and only occasionally go with their sons. Some don't even attend P.T.A. meetings or know the pediatrician very well. A's do all of those things. But B's are not impervious to the *feelings* in their family. They know when a daughter is acting flighty or a son, moody (or vice versa). They are sensitive to their wives' moods and feelings. One wife told me, "My husband knows when I'm about to get my period, for instance, before I do and he will usually do something special for me, like get up a little early and make me a breakfast tray without saying anything about it. He treats me as someone special, like I'm on a pedestal, I guess, but he never makes me feel silly. He's been like that from the first week we were married. Sometimes if I get snappy from fatigue or from a bad day at the office, he will say something like, 'What's the matter with *you?*' and push me out of the kitchen. But then that night, he'll be very tender and give me a rubdown."

The two types differ greatly in their views of how the family should respond to stress. A's are inclined to be protective of the children. B's let the kids know that they are expected to help in every way possible. If, for example, a working mother is under pressure at her job, a B husband will harness *the kids* who will end up taking over a large burden of the household chores. An A husband would be more likely to harness *himself,* and see to it that the house ran smoothly so that the kids didn't suffer from unusual tension. A connoisseur of feminist literature, A is aware that working mothers are often accused of neglecting their children. So, given a short-term breakdown in the maternal wing, he assumes that he must compensate. He and his wife, moreover, are proving something. They're proving that two working parents can be good parents. A wants to make sure his kids feel little stress even when there *is* stress.

The B husband has in mind something less complicated. The only war he is fighting is against inflation. So he takes one look at his healthy kids and tells them to get to work; their mother, he says, needs help.

Many women may think they want a B for a husband and, if they haven't got one, may crave one. But B's have their limitations too. They won't, for example, tolerate a woman who changes the ground rules on them, becomes an angry feminist after years of good-natured co-operation. The harmony of a B marriage hinges on the willingness of husband and wife to proceed on a "we're all in this together" basis. Intuitive sensitivities have guided them, and a B wife who comes home with a marriage contract is in for trouble.

Whatever he feels about his wife, B isn't likely to be patient with elaborate feminist rhetoric—or with most any kind of rhetoric. If pushed, he'll denounce the woman's movement—or any movement—as a congregation of lunatics.

Which means that a B wife, like an A husband, needs a sense of humor, a healthy ego, and a responsiveness to the traditional games of passion. If she falters in any of those areas, has an identity crisis at thirty-five, she's going to shake up the marriage. A

B wife would be wise to vent all her feminist spleen at the office and accept traditional nuances at home.

Type C: I came to call these husbands "supportive" but only with tongue in cheek. I've discovered that when the women I talked with labeled their husbands "supportive" what they usually mean is that he is "not totally hostile."

A "supportive" husband, in this generalized pattern, is a man who says it's okay for his wife to work, as long as she can keep up with everything else—the kids, the cooking, the house, and some sort of social life. A "supportive" husband obliges his wife to keep up an exhaustive façade—she must be a full-time wife and mother and a full-time "career woman" (that can mean anything from a Woolworth's cashier to a Woolworth's vice president).

Most women I talked with while researching this book are married to "supportive" husbands. Furthermore, they see their husbands as being fairly typical—"the way men are." Their husbands had after all agreed to their working, which for many women was a substantial concession in itself. C husbands don't hassle their wives constantly about returning to the hearth or quitting the job. But C wives pay a price for this freedom from harassment—in their willingness to overcompensate for their absence from the home by performing all normal domestic duties just as they always had.

"Supportive" husbands tend to have few legitimate complaints about their working wives. They are grateful for the extra income and are treated so well they wouldn't think of undermining their wives' efforts. In fact, most of them are so comfortable in their situation that they offer to "help" in some special way. One woman who commuted an hour each way to her job, arriving home at 6:30 every evening, told me that her biggest hassle was getting home and having her three children clamor for attention while she was bustling about in the kitchen making supper for everyone. Her husband usually arrived home a quarter to a half hour later than she did and collapsed in the living room. She'd been struggling with supper for two years in this way when her husband came up with an idea. He offered to make supper himself on Wednesdays. When I talked with her, he had been cooking Wednesday suppers for two months. I asked her early on in her interview how her husband felt about her working. "He thinks it's just fine," she told me. "In fact, he'd like it if I could do more in a way. I mean in my work if I can moonlight I make a tremendous amount of money, more than my salary on a per hour basis. He's really quite supportive."

I asked her *how* he was supportive, and she told me how she had struggled with the supper hours, and of his offer.

"It's just wonderful to know that I can have this little break in the middle of the week," she said. "I look forward to Wednesdays. I come home and make myself a drink and sit in the living room with the children, reading to them, or I sometimes let them watch the 'Electric Company' and I look at the paper. Then Tom calls us in and there it is . . . it may not be chicken divan but he's got the basics there. He's made meatloaf, spaghetti, roast beef, and things like that."

I asked her who cleaned up. "Oh well, we have a dishwasher and I always take care of that part," she said.

This woman, it must be understood, was very proud of her husband. So was he. She told me that at a recent party he had boasted of his cooking to some men and chided them about not doing the same thing. When I asked her if her husband did anything else around the house, she told me he took care of all the accounts (including her salary) and often took the kids someplace Saturday mornings so that she could get "the things done around the house that needed extra attention."

Some Type C husbands do even less. Yet they're called "supportive" because they offer moral support on the side. They serve as cheerleaders for wives who appreciate the encouragement, even if they don't get much team support. One woman who had brought up three children with a C husband cheering her on told me her story. She had, first of all, taken out eight years to rear them "properly," to get them started, and spend their baby years with them. Her husband was an electrical engineer, and she was a doctor. When she finally did go back to work, it was part time in a clinic, four days a week. In this way she didn't need any household help (a cleaning lady) and could still manage everything.

Her husband had always felt it was just "fine" if she wanted to maintain a practice and their life at home had not changed much at all since she had started. I asked her if there were any times of stress because of her work that made it essential for her to ask her husband for some extra help. The only thing she could think of was the four medical conventions she had attended in the past five years.

"I have to go to medical conventions every once in a while and I had never really thought about those when I decided to go back to work. I may be gone for a week at a time. My husband regarded that with a raised eyebrow in the beginning, and so I always asked him to come along. But he always said, 'No, thanks a lot.' In the first place medical conventions are still on the whole set up for doctors and their wives, with fashion shows for the non-participating spouse: my husband does not go in for fashion shows. He didn't want to be stuck in Miami or Atlanta for five days from morning to late in the afternoon for the privilege of seeing me. He doesn't like to go shopping; he can do any sight-seeing in one day and then what? So it never worked out.

"So the week before I go, I cook like crazy. I usually have seven dinners ready in the freezer, each with the appropriate label. In the morning, when my daughter goes to school, she goes to the freezer and takes that day's dinner out and then she comes home and there it says one hour at 325 degrees and that's all. Even though I'm gone, I'm still there managing the household. I have a clipboard and I write, for every day, what the food is and what should be done at what time, like if there is a piano lesson or flute lesson, or that night you have to do so and so . . . or empty the wastebasket or strip the beds, whatever has to be done.

"Sometimes when I do it and I'm tired, and a little frustrated, and I say for heaven's sake why do I have to do it? On the other hand, I don't really mind. Somehow, I have the feeling that that's part of my job. When you get married, although you don't find it out beforehand, you have a feeling that the husband takes care of the lawn and he'll make sure that it gets taken care of or the storm windows or whatever it is. And I make sure other things get done."

What, I wondered, were this woman's rewards? "My family is very proud of me," she told me. "My husband has told me that he is proud of my work and I know that he is. That I don't just sit around and play bridge or whatever."

Didn't she think she worked awfully hard for that praise? "Too many women are really little girls. They start to whine when the going gets tough. I've never complained to my husband and he would never expect me to."

What keeps a Type C husband afloat is his wife's assumption that he ought to be buoyed up. Certainly a C husband is not threatened by his wife's working, but neither is he challenged by her to change himself in any way. In this sense a woman who is married to Type C has to bear some of the responsibility for his lack of substantive support, his sometimes callow acceptance of his wife's work load, and his air of self-congratulation whenever he tells his wife she's doing a great job.

A Type C husband has never been shaken up. Which makes one wonder what would happen to him and to his marriage if he were. The answer to that is not altogether clear. Most women are reluctant to challenge the assumptions that allow them to get out of the house and be praised all the same.

The only way a C wife will ever change things is through her own initiative. She has, at any rate, one thing going for her that will help. Her husband, once he has been jolted to look honestly at the responsibilities he shares unevenly with his wife, will, in all probability, be contrite. Unlike a B, who has been working just as hard as his wife to keep the family going, a C has done almost nothing. He, of course, may be earning three times his wife's salary, providing his family with luxuries they gratefully appreciate, but his personal behavior has not been particularly nurturing to anyone.

The need for personal and family nurturing is the only argument these women have if they do decide to confront their husbands with the need for change. If they simply "complain" or insist that they are tired, they run the risk their husbands will tell them to quit. Which is, of course, what most of these women are afraid of in the first place. Nurturing may mean having a husband take a more active role in the children's lives so that, when both parents get home for dinner, the kids clamor for "daddy" while mother has a peaceful drink in the kitchen and tosses the spinach salad.

Many women married to "supportive" husbands seem to like it that way. So why advocate any changes at all? The issue is not so important for women who have been satisfied with a C husband for years, but women just starting out ought to be aware of the fact that a C marriage will put most of the working mother burdens onto her. A woman married to a man who insists he is not threatened by his wife's career, that he "supports" her efforts for an independent life, and will cheer her on as she cleans up the supper dishes and irons his shirts may need to call his bluff early on.

Type D: Otherwise known as *"the boys."* Any working mother married to one of *the boys* has got an impossibly demanding life.

A Type D husband can barely smother his anxiety and embarrassment at having a working wife. Every day is living agony for him, and he is sure the rest of the world thinks him a failure for having such a wife. He fears, moreover, that she is going to do something awful while she's out of the house.

Many of the boys are threatened by their working wives. None of them wanted one when they got married, and if they married a working woman, they expected her to quit and have babies as soon as the wedding and the living-room furniture were paid for. If she doesn't quit or eventually goes back to work, chances are the furniture never did get paid for and that his inadequacy is the reason why.

One of the boys never helps out at home unless the chore is something "manful," like painting the *outside* of the house or fixing an appliance. Because D's think domestic chores are demeaning, their wives work harder and harder as the number of children increase and the house has more rooms to be cleaned, more mouths to be fed, and more clothes to be laundered. Eventually all weekend time is devoured with wifely chores, which makes a D husband more and more withdrawn—he can't stand to see her work so hard, but he can't stand to help her. He's in a double bind and so is she.

D husbands usually take up a hobby or a sport so that they won't have to watch their wives work so hard, and because she's always busy, leave them alone for long hours. Some men take to the basement and work for years on cabinetry which they will eventually haul up as their contribution to the hard-working household. Others take to the golf course or bowling alley. Still others take to the local tavern and drink their way through the vision they need of themselves.

The boys seem a sad group, especially those whose wives are working because it is absolutely essential economically. Many D wives have encountered in their work lives a whole new set of priorities which makes life doubly difficult for their confused husbands. Even if their jobs are poorly paid drudgery, their ability to earn essential money fills many with a sense of self-worth that threatens their husbands even more than the fact of their working. Furthermore, they make friends at work who have the same problems they have and a camaraderie develops among them which threatens the already negligible intimacy of their marriages.

As a marital situation deteriorates, many families seek help from social workers or social service agencies. One woman who had reached this stage told me, "At first I thought this counseling was a help, but my husband was even more withdrawn afterwards. Because the message he got, you see, was that he ought to shape up. It didn't make any difference that I was also being made to listen to him in a different way. All he came away with was a deeper sense of inadequacy because he had to admit that he felt inadequate in front of me and this woman counselor. So he drinks when he's not working and he works whenever he can. We hardly see each other except as we pass in the halls."

Middle-class women married to one of the boys face an equally vicious battle, even if the weapons are more subtly concealed. A middle-class husband earning enough money to support a family reasonably well need not feel inadequate. He therefore assumes an air of suspicion and superiority in order to underline his wife's wavering self-confidence. The results are often disastrous. A middle-class D is likely to make a remark at a dinner party which undercuts his wife's professional abilities. "Sure, Rosie's a working mother. She's been teaching the same first grade for twelve years. One of these days she'll graduate herself . . . ha . . . ha."

Many women who stay married to a D for a long time develop problems with their own self-worth. They are apt, in the face of continual jabs at their worthiness, to buy the line. Eventually, even if they are earning good salaries, they believe that they are not very successful in life. They believe their husbands have more important jobs, more responsibilities, harder work, fewer leisure hours. One D wife told me, "I try to see to it that my husband gets the weekends free for himself. He works so hard all week that he needs a real break. I know I'd feel bad about my working if he couldn't have that time off."

If, however, a D husband is unable to sustain his wife's conviction that she is lucky to have him to care for, a D may lose his wife. This is one way working mothers get a bad name. Whenever one of the boys get evicted, he is mad as a hornet. He spreads stories all over town. The fallout from a D divorce is also harmful to neighborhoods, children, and the rest of the boys. Neighbors will, naturally, never know what really happened. Children will suffer from the bitterness that persists between their parents. And the rest of the boys will have to dig their trenches deeper in order to isolate their wives from that peculiar hazard—the divorced working mother who is happy, often for the first time in her adult life.

In summary, not every man obviously falls into an A, B, C, or D category. Not all of the boys have to stay in that league. Some supportive husbands do more than two to three helpful things a week, even though they still don't qualify for B status. And, although it's easy to poke fun at a priggish A, some well-meaning young husbands fall roughly into this category. Though the imperatives of feminism may have formed a virtual catechism in their lives—often because they've fallen in love with activist women—they somehow manage a sense of humor and an unwavering sense of themselves.

Finally, these stereotyped portraits are not meant to encourage further schism between disgruntled couples. My hope is that they will prove helpful to young couples who are about to become working parents. Once I began to notice that husbands could be grouped into more or less identifiable categories, I also realized that few men or women knew ahead of time what they were getting into when they initially decided to have children, yet both work. Forewarned is forearmed.

twelve

WHO'S AMBITIOUS?

Once I started working full time, I got increasingly self-confident. Whereas I had always had a very low opinion of myself, I seemed to feel better about my professional and therefore my everyday self. I personally feel that what I am doing has to fit into a much broader world. I began working professionally with a lot of men and women and liked the stimulation of people who were thinking in big terms. It certainly broadened by viewpoint and made me crystallize my thinking a lot more. I began to think that maybe I do have some original thoughts of my own that I can put into my own language. I had always felt a bit subservient to men and I began to see that I could work on a more equal basis. I found that when I disagreed with them, I could hold my own and hold onto my own ideas. That gave me a lot of self-confidence and independence really. A FIFTY-THREE-YEAR-OLD HIGH SCHOOL PRINCIPAL

Two major factors that working mothers deal with in relation to their work are: a deep struggle within the woman, and between women, over whether or not professional ambitions can coexist with children; and the problem of success, even modest success. How a woman balances her life so that she is both professional and mother—no longer torn between deep commitments to both, but satisfied with her role in each.

Most women, I found, have difficulty working out these issues alone—because they can't react to them in a vacuum. They are married, and find themselves organizing work and children in their lives in a way that corresponds to the amount of emotional and physical support they receive from their husbands. This prohibits many women from examining their professional yearnings for what they are. This is just as true for women who *seem* to be very ambitious as for women who *seem* not to be.

Most women are anxious to separate their own accomplishments from their husbands'. They are also anxious to assure people that they do not "compete" with their husbands. Women find it difficult, nonetheless, to separate what they want for themselves from what they want for their families.

The question has to be asked: How do working mothers react to ambition? Are they just as determined to do anything, go anywhere, for a job as their male counterparts at the office? What effect does being a working *mother*, a wife, and household manager have on a woman's professional drive?

Whenever I asked a working mother if she considered herself ambitious, I usually got a quick and definitive "No!" Yet, I discovered, to admit ambition is one thing, to be ambitious is another. If a woman told me she did not consider herself ambitious, yet she was chief administrator of a metropolitan health clinic, I had to decide whether she was rejecting ambitiousness as a label or had failed to grasp something important about her work.

Women's often expressed distaste for ambition has little to do with actual striving and/or capacity for success. But it *does* have to do with the interplay of domestic and professional lives, and with the powerful emotional legacy of several hundred years of female domesticity.

Why *are* working mothers so reluctant to "achieve," and why are they so timid about admitting it when they have? From my interviews, several possible answers suggest themselves.

First, working mothers have been reluctant to move out of a traditionally feminine willingness to settle into middle management positions; they have passively waited for promotions instead of lobbying for them; they have doggedly followed a tendency to bury themselves in specialities, often undemanding ones, which men rarely covet.

I was sitting in the kitchen of a young couple in New York City late one evening. It was after midnight, and I had spent several hours with the working mother of this family. Now I had joined them for some wine and some tired talk.

"I wonder how many women you will find," the young man asked me, "who will insist they have actively pursued some sort of white-collar position, agressively?"

I asked him what he meant.

"I mean the kind of job leverage options that executives, male executives, use in order to climb up the ladder," he said. "I've worked for three different companies, for example, in the past eight years. The reason I've worked for three, instead of staying with one and working my way steadily, though *slowly*, up the ladder, is that I knew if I wanted to get ahead quickly I had to make some jumps. I could get promotions, be seen as a more valuable commodity, if I hustled about and got job offers from competitive companies. Sitting still in one firm is rarely seen by the guys upstairs as very ambitious, aggressive behavior. They'll forget you're there after a while. So you've either got to go to them and say, 'I've got this offer from Company X and I'm debating whether or not to take it,' or you have to simply go so they will see you as a man on the rise. A few years later, they may try to buy you back . . . at a much higher price."

White-collar aggressiveness is obviously something women need to know more about. In Boston, Simmons College has just begun offering a master's program for women in management. One of the novel components of its twelve-month program is a study of "male corporate behavior," a course designed to help women compete for jobs in the face of a male executive tradition that honors at least one important premise—keep women out.

On the whole, of course, companies *have* been very successful in keeping women out. According to the U. S. Department of Labor, Employment Standards Administration, only 5 per cent of all women workers are in managerial positions, and less than 4 per cent are salaried managerial workers (1971). Labor Department statistics also show that nearly seven out of ten men—but only two out of ten women—who are salaried managers earned $10,000 or more in 1970, while one out of ten men—but only one out of a hundred women—earned $25,000 or more.

"White-collar" women are not alone in getting short-suited when it comes to pay or authority. In 1970, for instance, "blue-collar" women represented 21 per cent of the membership of organized labor. Yet they held only 4.7 per cent of all union leadership positions. Why? *U.S. News and World Report* came up with four basic reasons, as of 1972.

First, caring for a house and holding down a full-time job left many women little free time for union activities or meetings, most often held at night.

Second, women tend to choose male spokesmen within their own unions, a trend attributed to "a social conditioning that has perpetuated a lack of self-confidence and lack of confidence in other women."

Third, their husbands have not wanted them to get involved with unions. Nor, for that matter, have husbands wanted them to work.

Fourth, many women are afraid of reprisals if they become "too aggressive" on the job or in the union. They are afraid of failure caused by lack of self-confidence. They are afraid of losing male protection if they "relinquish their passive roles."

One woman, a legislative representative of the Clothing Workers, added, "Traditionally, the role played by women rank and file has been a subdued one. Unlike many professional women, they often have lacked the income to afford household help, which is one of the reasons our union pushed to set up day-care centers."

Among *working mothers*, I'd assumed, I'd find a stronger determination for professional advancement, and a more mature self-confidence. Women, I reasoned, who were working full time, had taken on the responsibility of raising children, caring for a home, and sticking with a marriage—these women had to be held together with a solid sense of self-worth and determination.

Many women, for example, told me they "felt more grown up" than their husbands. But the same women reacted to male or other hostility by closing some theretofore vulnerable gates, retreating behind an all but impregnable wall of stoicism, their own psychic survival. Yet despite their obvious competence in protecting themselves from unreasonable outside attacks, they seem to suffer from a chronic internal fragility which allows them to penetrate the working world *only so far*.

One woman told me, "My method has always been to do what I need to accomplish my goals, with as little tension as possible. I hate scenes and I hate confrontations, and the few I've had have shattered *me* probably more than the other person."

She seemed to speak for many women. Women, I found, had little "white-collar aggressiveness" as a group. Women tend to stay with one company most of their professional lives—unless their husbands are transferred out of the area. They wait for promotions. They choose specialties within their own professions, and bury themselves in their own private areas of expertise—where no one can attack them or compete with them.

Another woman, a newspaper reporter, said, "If I had to do it all over again, I think I'd have learned early the business side of my profession in some way. I never did. I don't know anything about production or marketing or management. The male colleagues I started out with do. They made it their business to spend time and get involved in all the departments here. Now the men who started with me are running this huge operation, with experience in every department. I'm still turning out feature articles for the 'living' page. I'm paid more than when I started out, but not that much more, and I think those little raises through the years have been my poisoned apple. I took them so gratefully."

Working mothers tend to down play the value of their work. Most women acknowledge the transcendent value of their husband's work. "My husband's work is vital, more important than my own, an important factor in the way I view priorities in our house," said a teacher, the wife of a physicist.

Many insist that their husband's work is more creative. "His talent makes all the difference. No matter how many books I write, how much I earn, I know that my husband is much more creative than I am and that prevents us from really being competitive," said an economist married to an architect.

Some women feel that their husband's work is needed more in the world than their own. "My husband is a doctor. He saves lives. There's no question that his work is indispensable and my own is peripheral," a journalist and mother of four told me.

Many women prize their husband's work more than their own simply because he earns more. "I suppose if I could earn $20,000 a year, I might think differently, but in our house my husband's work comes first," said a secretary at a law firm, married to an insurance broker.

Several women told me they valued their husband's work more than their own simply because he was a man and therefore had to worry more about his work. "My husband, because he's male, is taking his work seriously in a way I don't have to. He's always got to worry about his image as a provider and I can afford to sit at home and think over the value of this and that. He's got to think of making money—the ambition thing of realizing his masculine potential in a worldly sense," said a writer married to a college administrator.

Middle-class women who do not feel that their salaries are vital to the family tend to emphasize this ambivalence over the value of their work because, they say, there is no urgency about it.

Karin is a free-lance writer. Her husband is a professor. She has written for national magazines and newspapers and clearly loves her work, when she works. But she does not see her career as a viable means of support or as a major contribution to the family. The money she earns is always put into "frills" or "a trinket for our living room. . . . I like to see my work in the form of some bauble in our house and I can point to it and say to myself, 'That was the article on this or that.' I'd hate to see my salary get gobbled up by the gas or electric company." Karin is a talented writer, but she prefers not to think of this as a serious component in the family plan. When I asked her if she ever felt ambitious she said:

"Am I ambitious? Now I'm sure I'm going to come down on the unpopular side here. One thing that's important to say is I couldn't survive as a free-lance writer were it not for the great salary coming from *mon mari*. Nor would I really want to. I would want the security of an office. Sometimes I see myself essentially as a person who can't cope, who hasn't proven herself and probably never will. In certain ways. The up and down, the bad scenes of free-lance writing are only what I deserve.

"About a year ago I was going through a phase which I am only just getting out of. I looked about me and realized that all the people I knew had done things like work their way through college, or they took civil service exams when they were eighteen years old and worked in the bowery or some crummy part of New York all summer long in an un-air-conditioned office. Some people held down two jobs. This made me feel terrible.

"I felt terribly jealous. I find myself avoiding work. Why don't I do it? I have the time. I adore the field. I love having these assignments. I love to earn money. I love to see my name in print, and I love the push I get when I have sat down for an hour and I have worked hard and my back aches and I've written something good. I love it!

"My husband, David, went to law school, a hard thing to do. He did very well and now he teaches. That's different from this untrained namby-pamby subjective here today and gone tomorrow work that I do. I like to think that if I had gone to law school I would feel differently. But I never went.

"I have a Ph.D. neurosis. I feel that, well, this is such a joke among people who know me that they tell me, 'A Ph.D. is nothing. I'll make you a Ph.D., Karin. I'll write one right here on this paper towel and you can have it.' Nothing will remove from me the idea that a Ph.D. represents a solid ongoing respectable objective. Even if I had a Ph.D. in Shakespeare, I'd probably say, 'But that doesn't make me Shakespeare.' This is a focus of great neurotic conflict for me. I think of it as representing the cod liver oil of the mind. It's unpleasant and it's worthy. I think this is what men do—take the cod liver oil."

Karin envied men with a Ph.D., assuming that the degree and education behind it would make a difference in her professional view of herself. Yet women with graduate degrees and years of special training, I found, still underplayed their professional significance.

Among the women doctors I interviewed, for example, all had chosen a specialty likely to be less demanding than their husband's work. They rarely became surgeons. More often they were anesthesiologists, dermatologists, allergists, pediatricians, or gynecologists. Most of them worked a four-day week or a part-time day. Their husbands did not. Many of them had doctors for husbands. Their husbands were surgeons, neurologists, psychiatrists, radiologists, or specialists in other demanding fields. Furthermore, all of the husbands combined a private practice with at least one academic appointment. The men had written widely in professional journals. The women had not. The men earned more money, worked longer hours, and enjoyed far more status than their wives.

Why? Because the wives knew that someone had to stay home some of the time and see to the children. They knew that someone had to have a more relaxed schedule in order to "be there" when the children needed emotional relief. They knew they could not seriously suggest that their husbands sacrifice some small share of professional ambition in order to take on some share of parental responsibility.

These women had to put up with incredible opposition and discrimination in medical school as well as residency. They were "fighters," in the sense that they saw themselves making inroads for other women. Even so, they could go *only so far.*

"If you had to do it all over again, what would you change?" I asked them. Several insisted they would finish all their training before having children. They would have "gone into research," which meant they would have had more rigorous schedules in the beginning. How would that have affected them at home? They would have "waited and had their children later."

No one said, "I would have worked something out with my husband so that child care was divided more evenly." "I would have asked my husband to help more." "I would have asked him if he wanted to stay home."

An underlying fear among these women doctors was that they would "lose their femininity" if they succumbed completely to their professional calling. They saw their maternal roles as visible proof that they were really just like other women. Having broken into the most solid male bastion—medicine—they had to separate their sexual identity from the white suit they worked in. Many of them had gone through years of training associating mostly with men. Now that their training was over, they wanted to become accepted by other women. Living in neighborhoods where most women were housewives, they felt a painful isolation, sought to compensate for their "masculine" profession through little demonstrations of their feminine nature—such as taking over a car pool, holding special birthday parties for children in the neighborhood, or taking part in neighborhood social activities.

Choosing a less demanding specialty, not getting involved in research, working part time, are ways in which women assure themselves and the rest of the world that their husbands really do wear the pants in the family—that their husbands are "real men" and they "real women."

The Educational Testing Service released a 214-page report, "Women, Men and the Doctorate," in which they cite marriage and motherhood as the "main impediments to the professional advancement of women with doctoral degrees." The report goes on to say, "Often women describe a vicious circle. Women with young children sought part-time work. Men with full-time positions received the grants, published the research and got the promotions. Then by the time women were able to return to full-time work, their field (or men in their field) had passed them by and there was nothing to do but take the lesser jobs. . . . Because of the difference in the pattern of their private lives," the report says, "12 per cent of the women but only 2 per cent of the men did not go directly into the job market immediately after being awarded doctorates."*

Living within the boundaries of carefully defined sex roles seems to be one more reason women find to play down their professional self-esteem and drive. Fatigue is another factor. Handling two jobs is tiring and fatigue often precludes ambition. Barbara Walters and other women who've made a huge success of their careers say, "We have to be better, work harder, than anyone else." But I can't forget all the women I've talked with who have no such goals, and are still working very hard with no let-up. Not even at their camp grounds while on vacation.

Another inhibitor of ambition among working mothers is the problem of geographical mobility and the strong likelihood that they will follow their husband's lead in moving from one location to another. This is especially true during the first fifteen years of marriage, a period in life when many men "on the move" are literally moving from one corporate headquarters to another.

Because husbands usually earn more money, it makes sense for families to follow them across the country—more so than to stay with or follow a potential move on the part of a mother. It makes sense up to a point—the point where a woman realizes that the reason she is not making as much money as her husband is because she is uprooted from her job periodically, just as she is about to advance. Over and over again she starts, and only rarely does her own career dovetail with her husband's.

As I've suggested elsewhere in this book, the explanation most working mothers offer for the modest progress they've made in their careers is their unwillingness to make demands on their husbands—in the home or at the office. Their husband's career comes first, the family comes second, and their own career is a distant third.

* The New York *Times*, January 6, 1975, Gene I. Maeroff.

Many women, recognizing these things and accepting their inevitability, steer clear of any full-time commitment and adopt what might be called the "chocolate cake" thesis. They are working mothers, yet their work is part time, an arrangement which they feel allows them "the best of both worlds," the "chocolate cake" of life.

These women told me they had learned something from their husbands. They had seen how one-sided their husband's lives were, and they wanted no part of it. Women who worked part time or who had jobs they could work at in their homes often speak of their unwillingness to sell themselves to corporate life. For some women—self-confident, talented or skilled—part-time work is fully satisfying, and when they speak of the richness of their life, they are believable. They're the lucky few.

Gretchen is a free-lance photographer and part-time college instructor. Although she works hard—producing numerous photographic essays for magazines and newspapers every year—she is careful never to work too hard, at either her homemaking or her various jobs. I asked her to describe for me a perfect day in her life:

"A perfect day would be a day in which I—well sometimes when I sit down to read and I really sink in to the point where I almost feel like I'm in a yoga trance because I'm so deeply into it, my mind is not rushing elsewhere, I think this is one of the good things that life is and I want it to be more often. One of my itchy terrors sometimes when I wake up is, 'What am I going to do today? Do I have something to do? Is it something that I have to do but I don't want to do it?' There ought to be some nice combination of activity, solidity, depth, thrill, and inspiration. That's what I'd like for work. I'd like the children to come home from school and we'd go apple picking. I'd like to cook a wonderful meal that could be delicious and exciting and bizarre. Then I'd like some nice person we both liked a lot to come over for drinks. Then I'd like to work for about three hours. Then I'd like to watch television, make love, and go to bed. In other words, even my ideal is quite divided. I wouldn't like to see myself at work nine to five."

Gretchen, and many women like her, take great pleasure in this not always predictable combination of life at home, life at work. But the "thrill and depth," the chance to name her own hours and wages that Gretchen enjoys, is rarely available, say, to a computer programmer or a bank teller.

Part-time employment for women *or men* at any time of life, particularly when they have young children to care for, ought to be taken seriously. But the issue of ambition should not be glossed over by the "chocolate cake" way of life.

Mothers who work part time often have a very hard time of it. They rarely earn enough money to cover all their expenses—an important factor in the way women value paid, as opposed to volunteer, work. They still have the primary role in household management and childrearing—their husbands earn much more and are reluctant to assume more burdens. Most important, their work may be just as hard as it is for women with full-time jobs. Few jobs, part-time workers learn, are ever "half-time." So they are tired, frustrated, and often as anxious as any unemployed housewife—how far, they wonder, could they go in the world of work?

They know how well they can do their jobs—so suspect that, but for their family obligations, they would be accomplishing as much or more than other men (or women) in their professions. How can they prove their competence, they wonder, when they are continually reining themselves in?

Mothers with part-time jobs tend to value their work and themselves less than mothers who work full time. They take themselves less seriously than they take their husbands, a condition already epidemic among women across the board.

"You don't make that much money in the end, but I never saw it as a money-making proposition. I see it more as a recreation than anything else," one part-time librarian told me. She told me that her husband rarely thinks about her work. "He just doesn't take it very seriously. He's just wound up in what he does himself."

These women have a greater tendency to regard the money they earn as an isolated pocket of income, a lucky night at bingo. None of these women used the total of their pay, along with their husband's, as a basis from which to deduct the cost of child care and household services. They deducted the cost of those items from *their* income—and thus reduced its value further, as a drain against family resources.

Part-time work is often regarded by husbands and wives as "keeping a finger in the pie." It was not, for most people I discovered, an answer to balancing out a life made up of children, household activity, and work.

Nobody likes to look at the consequences. And for good reason. Many women, of course, simply continue to live out their lives stifling their ambition, never knowing or asking themselves what they might have done or might have wanted to do. The neurotic repercussions of their lives are in the psychiatric textbooks—more women suffer from depression and neurosis in middle age they say.

Some women, however, are moved to a reawakening. Sensing that motherhood and all the repercussions of motherhood are insufficient for a lifetime, they realize they want something else as well. Although they have enjoyed being a homemaker and mother, they have continually lived with an inner curiosity about themselves . . . how well, they want to know, would they do in the world of work? Could they have been good at something, something else?

So they want to find out; they want to test their wings. Not long ago, we saw a rash of magazine articles about women leaving their children and husbands to pursue their own lives—and careers. We haven't seen the follow-through, however. We've read nothing since about how those women find their lives, divorced from their families. Their marriages may have been unsatisfying but, had they been more honest about their ambitions prior to their marriages, they might still be living with the children they bore.

Jane had spent thirteen years raising four children, putting her husband through graduate school and tending to their household. At thirty-one she took a part-time job at a newspaper; just some copy editing, just to pass the time. Two years later her life had changed drastically.

"One of the great moments in my life was the rush of excitement I felt when I first realized how determined I was to be a 'professional' and a *success*. For a time I went around dumbstruck. I had the feeling I had shed nearly thirty years of conditioning. I had opened up, made functional, a part of me—a main artery clogged from disuse.

"I'm thinking of the little jobs, the kind we women are apt to pick up from time to time in our desire to be good citizens . . . a politician asks us to canvass the neighborhood; someone else gets us involved with the P.T.A. and we end up being someone's chief fund raiser. The small accolades we get from these 'jobs well done' are pleasing but only momentarily, and they have the odd effect, I now believe, of reinforcing the very nonprofessional aimlessness they routinely exploit.

"I accepted any praise for any job at all with pleasure. It made me feel good to have someone tell me I had done something well, even if we were talking about a chore no more complicated than addressing a few envelopes, making a series of telephone calls, or making arrangements for a white elephant sale.

"I might have become addicted to community gratefulness if someone hadn't made the mistake of paying me a small amount of money somewhere along the way.

"It took me a while to realize what was happening. I lingered over each work experience as if I were watching a twenty-four-hour movie. Fortunately, when the climax of the film arrived, I was not out at the concession stand. I was in my seat staring with wide open eyes.

"I can still remember one cold autumn morning when I walked out my front door lugging a briefcase. It was 6:30 A.M. My husband, bathrobed and unshaven, kissed me good-bye, then shuffled back into the warm house to get the kids ready for school before he left for his own job. I was headed for Connecticut to do a story. As I reached the turnpike and felt the car hum into fourth gear, I felt my blood rush. I was alone, watching the sun hit the New England foliage, and life seemed much too grand to be real. I can remember shaking, shivering, with nervous release. I knew where I was going and it wasn't just Connecticut. I was going to work.

"I was going to work every day of my life. For the first time in years I was consciously thinking about a professional future. The idea that I was to take myself seriously, and actively search for writing or other editorial assignments changed me drastically. It forced me to redesign my whole attitude towards myself. I wasn't just a housewife who dabbled with the pen. I was going to earn a living wage. I was going to write any damn thing I could get paid for. I was going to learn to be a 'professional.' I felt ruthless, aggressive, ambitious. By the end of my day in Connecticut, I had good reason to be.

"I stood in an office waiting room. I had been sent by my editor to interview a prominent New England politician. When I was finally ushered into the man's office, I caught a long stare from a sour-looking man who evidently had no memory of having agreed to the interview. He looked me up and down, smirked, and said, "Okay, sweetie, how do you want it?"

"I felt like someone had just spilt soup in my lap. When I was finished with him, he was red-faced and I was ready to return to the front lines."

Some women are not as able as Jane to find a job or the skill to match. Many women, once they try to get into the world of work on a full-time basis, find their vision of themselves, newly arrived at, seems unreal.

Through their husbands, they've lived at the edge of a world of competent people with experience and special skills. These women know, have absorbed, a lot, but not enough of what it takes to succeed in those circles. For years they have been living with self-esteem through association—they have been treated with stylized respect by their husbands' peers. A sort of professional code exists between successful men—thou shalt always treat a "wife of" with papal awe. Very polite social evenings—year after year—have allowed these wives to feel that their opinions were worth something . . . professionally. But they're not, when the chips are down. So the wife of a manager of a large chain of department stores assumes, at forty-five, that she can take over the women's dress department. But she doesn't know how to make all sorts of daily judgments that make the difference between a good season or a bad.

This woman might then either retreat and recite the litany of precepts about the importance of a woman staying home with her family; or she will persevere, learn the hard way. In the end, even then, some will be totally defeated.

No woman should insist that she has the "chocolate cake" of life—the best of both worlds—when she clearly faces a dozen insecure moments a day. Although it is true that women who have really found themselves, know their abilities and how to use them in both worlds can find the best and sustain it—many women don't.

Perhaps the most offensive consequence of women finding themselves late in life, after they have had children and "settled themselves" into a family life, is that they take on qualities of mind and action that are ugly and disastrous for everyone—themselves, their families, and their peers who have put up with them. Such women move briskly into the world of work, establish a "power" base, and quickly lose all sense of perspective. How we all hate the woman at a dinner party who lets it be known how hard she has worked all day, how terrific her work is, how pleased she is with herself, and, by implication, how disastrous the lives of all the other women there must be. Women who have just put the kids to bed cringe at her pomposity.

Patricia Sexton writes of such women in her book *The Feminized Male:*

> Because of the tortured path they must follow, women who make it in the man's world are often odd and misshapen. Many a shrike is found in their numbers. To get anywhere on their own, women often must work and fight harder than men. Many become extremely marginal and isolated. While some of the best rise on performance and talent, many others rise on sheer gall and aggression. These tend to be the shrews, whose shrill assaults on others earn them their bad reputations.†

Ambition is a heady brew, which needs to be recognized when, and as soon as, it occurs. The longing for success, however, is no substitute for skill and experience. Women, mothers, who have deferred, or repressed, their job aspirations need to proceed cautiously, to weave into the fabric of their lives a tolerable mixture of labor and love, pride of accomplishment, and respect for the interests and achievements of others.

Once ambition becomes accepted as one of the womanly virtues, everyone stands to benefit—wives and mothers because they need be ashamed no longer of their lusting for the stars; husbands because that passion will no longer come as a disorienting surprise; children because they will no longer have to range uncertainly between the parental poles of fatherly aggression and maternal warmth. And, of course, they (these children) will have less trouble adjusting to the fact of ambition in their own adult lives.

† Random House, 1969, p. 156.

thirteen

SOME NEW ADVICE

Sigmund Freud once said that after thirty years of studying the female soul, he still didn't know what women want. I'm a woman, a mother, a wife, and a professional career woman, and I don't know what we women want. Who does? Maybe we just want too much.
A THIRTY-SIX-YEAR-OLD CLINICAL PSYCHOLOGIST

One constant theme of this book has been that working mothers need to face their many difficulties confidently. Most books written for parents attempt to impart a self-confident approach toward childrearing, and they can be terrific fallbacks for the moments of indecision most parents face each day. These books are full of common sense and the benefit of a great deal of grandmotherly hindsight.

If, as I've argued, most commonplace advice to working mothers is based on faulty or outmoded assumptions and a fundamental hostility to the principles of equality, where then do working mothers go for sensible answers to their many daily conundrums? And what sort of advice would they get from such oracles? To the extent that the collective wisdom and perceptions of the more than two hundred women I've interviewed add up to a coherent position on these matters, the following hypothetical questions and answers may prove a partial answer.

I felt terrific about being a working mother and going back to work when my baby was one month old; but I have real doubts now. I miss out on a lot of his life, the small discoveries he makes when he opens his eyes from a nap and discovers how to touch his mobile. For every month I'm away, will I be more and more excluded from his world?

You're right, you're going to miss out on some of your child's shining moments. The first time you send your preschooler off to nursery school, then kindergarten, first grade, you will realize that he or she is going to experience some precious or formative moments with other people—a realization that every mother has. On the whole, however, you will get the best of your baby's formative years. As the months go on, you can build up more and more time with your child, until you feel more confident and closer in touch with him. No one can replace you, something your baby will realize very soon. He'll save up the best times for you when you get home—and, of course, the worst too.

My husband and I thought our baby had adjusted beautifully when I went back to work six weeks after he was born. Now at sixteen months, he cries and holds out his arms to be picked up as soon as the sitter comes and I leave for work. Does this happen to everyone? Should I quit now, before it gets worse?

It happens to a lot of people, especially with a baby that age. He is testing you and he will continue to test you, until he's roughly thirty-two.

The worst thing you can do is quit now. If you do, he'll expect you to give in next time too. But you *can* help him feel he doesn't have to test you. Make sure you and your husband spend a lot of extra time with him; and particularly that your husband has moments with him *alone*. A baby with *two* parents to test may tire of it or lose interest.

Leave for work in a confident manner. Don't stiffen or show that leaving him hurts you as much as it does him. Assure him that you will be back at the same time as always—and then make sure you are. Leave before your husband in the morning, if the baby seems more strongly attached to you at this stage.

Finally, make sure your child-care help knows you are confident you are doing the right thing. The only conflict in the house at this time should be within the baby, and he will relax more if he observes that he doesn't have to worry—if he doesn't sense other people are worried.

One more thing: don't read any pediatric literature for at least six months unless you see red spots on the baby's stomach.

My husband commutes one hour to his job in the city and I'm offered a job that will keep me at least thirty minutes' distance from my three small children. Is that too far away from my children? Should I take the job?

The thirty minutes isn't bad if the drive is an easy one, but a wiser alternative, if it were possible, would be to move closer to your husband's job, perhaps so each of you were only thirty minutes from work. Then you can share emergency calls and you will not be worried constantly that you are the *only* one who can come to the children's rescue.

If you can't move, talk with your husband about ways he can ease what will prove a huge burden—perhaps altering his work schedule, so that he can take over some cooking, shopping, or other day-to-day household chores.

My children are nine and twelve and get home from school at 3 P.M. I've always had a housekeeper on duty to greet them and watch over them until I get home at 5:30 but now they say they are old enough to be home without her. I may be old fashioned but the thought of them home alone bothers me. Should I worry?

Sure, but some children, much younger than yours, get to be very reliable "latch key" kids, trustworthy and reasonably secure. If you're thinking of doing it, ask yourself how mature the children are; how well do they get along together; how accessible is your house to emergency help; where, in your neighborhood, you can count on someone if emergency help is needed. Your children may prove very capable and reward you with their efforts to be helpful and independent.

Some nine-year-old children care for their four-year-old siblings better than some professional housekeepers do. Age does not seem to be the crucial factor in determining a person's ability to cope with independence and responsibility.

If you do decide to let your children take care of themselves for the few hours before you get home, try to structure their time—at least to some extent. Give them a schedule of things they ought to do while you are at work—finishing their homework, emptying the dishwasher, calling you at the office to report in, setting the table, and the like. Then set some careful rules, straightforward enough for them to follow, but not so overbearing they will feel you don't trust them.

My husband says that since he's earning $30,000 a year and I earn $7,000, his job is more important to the family than mine and should be treated that way. He's right of course, but we have three children and I feel like a rag because my children take so much of my time and he isn't interested in any child care. Should I quit?

Only his arithmetic is right and yes, I think you should quit—pampering him. Salary isn't the only measure of the "worth" of jobs in your family. If your work is a vital part of your life, if it gives you pleasure, a sense of self-worth, you certainly shouldn't give it up. Try to make your husband understand that you share an equal right to aspire to professional success; that your life is as important as his; that you are *both* the parents of your children; that they *need* a father, not simply a wage earner.

I'm working at a plant with a day-care center, but I've heard so many bad things about day care I'm reluctant to try it. I have a three-year-old home with a baby-sitter, and I think she would enjoy playing with more friends her own age. But day care all day?

You may have the best form of child care in the world right there in your plant and you shouldn't be afraid of it. Check it out, look around, spend some time there with the staff, watch how they are with small children, talk to other parents who use it, read what you can about day-care centers. If you spot flaws, remember it's your day-care center, and you can help improve it.

Day care all day may mean your child will spend less time away from you than she does now with the baby-sitter. The fact that your day-care center is located near your place of work means that you may visit your child for lunch, take a coffee break with her, pick her up sooner at the end of the day, and give her the assurance she may need by showing her where you go to work every day—even better, taking her on the bus or in the car *with you*. I'll bet she'll love it. But do your homework first.

We're both working parents and have two small children, one nine months and the other two and a half years. I want my husband and I to take a vacation this year away from them, for just one week. I feel we run ourselves ragged all year and it would be good for our souls. But my husband is balking. How can I convince him that parents have rights too, and it will be good for the whole family if we have some private time?

Although I would agree that it is very important to have some private time with your husband, it may be a difficult time for you both to leave the children—when they are that young. If you go away now, you may frighten them, or, at the least, jeopardize the trust they've learned to have in you and your comings and goings. Their sense of time is confused and it may be difficult for them to understand that it really is for only one week. Many mothers who have tried such a vacation tell me that they pay for it on return as their children, under three or four, suffer prolonged separation problems for weeks or months later.

Maybe you could take a baby-sitter with you on your vacation so that you and your husband feel free enough to take part of each day away alone and on adult activities.

One other solution: Try separate vacations. Many working parents who have tried this say that the quiet, private time to reflect and relax without any schedules to meet, without being answerable to anyone's moods or desires, is the best vacation of all. And the kids are never left without one of you.

What do you do about vacations, in the summer or during the school year—when children are home, with time to burn?

Most working mothers plan summers and week-long vacations carefully. That means day camps, an occasional overnight camp for older children, or special trips and supervised entertainment during shorter vacations. Find other working mothers with the same problem and see if you can't work trade-offs. Barring that, you've got to count on the training you've given your children—to be self-sufficient, make friends on their own, and schedule their time wisely. A lot of kids will tell you what they want to do. Barring a trip to Disneyland, you might be able to accommodate them.

Most important, remember that these vacations come at the same time yearly, so it's one other item the kids have got to adjust to. One more reason for chosing the neighborhood you live in carefully, if you're a working mother.

As for the shorter vacations, Christmas and the like, let the kids, provided they're not too young (under seven or eight), join the adult world for a while. Let your children stay up past their bedtime, even if they sleep later in the morning. Take them to plays, movies, and out to dinner at night. They'll get some extra time with you, benefit from some special occasions that nonworking mothers provide in the daytime, and probably feel superior to their peers for the privilege.

No matter how well I arrange things, I feel guilty every time my child is in a play and I can't attend, or gets invited to a birthday party that some mother has organized in a big way. How do working mothers give their children the same kind of attention other kids get?

Chances are, you're responding to a traditional view of the problem. Don't expect to give your children the same kind of life you had, or that your next-door neighbor feels she must provide. You can give your children the love and attention they need without playing permanent mother hen. If you're feeling guilty over the birthday party coming up for your six-year-old, the party that's going to occur the same day you have to meet a deadline at the office, ask your husband if he can't handle this one, or postpone the party till Saturday.

I live in a community with no day care and, I'm told, it's practically impossible to get good household help here. I want to go back to work. How do other women in the suburbs break free?

The greatest impediment to women who want to return to work is their assumption that they won't be able to find a good mother substitute. No matter what you've been told, advertise and be ruthless in interviewing—follow up on résumés, insist on making a decision only after you have talked it over with your husband (not while the applicant is still sitting in the living

room); arrange a trial period, and tell yourself, daily, that the
process is worth it.

If you find you are still at a loss, move. Although it takes a lot
of courage to uproot a family and start all over again, a move may
well prove more tolerable than the frustration you're living with
now.

*My wife is a working mother and we have an infant boy, three
months old. Since her pregnancy she has been emotionally high
strung and now she suffers from depressions and guilt feelings. I'm
perfectly prepared to do my part and I want to be an equal
parent, but I don't know how to convince her that she ought to
stop worrying. What should I do?*

Your wife's emotional upheaval is common. It's a time most
parents have to live through and chalk up to experience. Stretch
your patience as far as it will go but try to help her gain self-
confidence in her new role. Women often revert to very childish
behavior shortly after childbirth, possibly because historically
women have been pampered during childbirth and postpartum
blues. A lot of the pampering is needed; a lot of it is prolonged
unnecessarily.

Make her understand that you are just as responsible for the life
of that baby as she is. It's your baby too, so take a lot of initiative
in caring for it and for the house. She'll probably be relieved. One
cause of her depression may be her overwhelming sense that she is
now burdened with the baby's care—forever. Moreover, she will
benefit from her work as soon as she stops feeling the way her
grandmother told her to.

*I love my life as a working mother but I have a problem: When
do working mothers and their husbands find time for sex? I'm
too tired at night; too rushed in the morning; and I'm at my office
all afternoon. Life is not much different over the weekend and
once a week, four times a month, is not our idea of a loving
marriage.*

Ask yourself why you are so tired every night. Are you getting
the kind of support you need from your family? Are you the only
one who is so tired? If you're both tired you need to make some
changes in your life-style. If only you are exhausted, try some new
household arrangements with your husband. Connive with him

for evenings when the children are in bed on time and you have nothing scheduled. And decide what is truly important in your life. A dirty house might be a small price to pay for a relaxed, loving sex life with your husband.

I am worried that my three-year-old daughter will be confused by the different number of adults who take care of her—her parents, the afternoon baby-sitter, the morning nursery school teachers. Will she have too many different adult expectations placed on her? We're all different personalities.

As long as you are confident that the adults who care for her are cheerful, warm, responsible, and like children, your daughter will probably benefit from the many exposures. She may grow up to be more flexible and relaxed with other people. I wouldn't worry unless you see signs that one of the adults is not working out well —then find out what is wrong with the adult, not your child. Mothers find that as long as the adults taking care of a child don't change very often, so that the child can learn to trust the same faces, the number is less important. Better that your daughter have five different adults taking care of her all year than that the scene shift from one housekeeper to another month after month.

My husband is a salesman and gone for at least one week out of every month. Although I work, I end up getting more child-care responsibilities than he does. How can I help him to be more of an equal parent when the schedule already precludes constant participation?

The first twenty-four hours after a husband returns usually produce a lot of tension as he tries to work himself back into the family. A good solution is for him to take over a large portion of child-care responsibility immediately, often to the exclusion of the wife altogether. This way, children don't cling to their mother while eying their father suspiciously—and a wife can catch her breath, have some day time to herself, and get revved up for an evening with her husband that will be child-free, grown-up.

Equal parenting doesn't always have to mean sharing on a quid pro quo basis. It does mean being willing and unafraid to take over completely whenever it makes sense to do so.

All of my children want me to take a bigger part in their school activities, the way other mothers do. They tell me they wish I didn't work. My husband thinks it's fine that I work but I don't know how to convince my children that I can't do everything.

Even if you were home all the time, you probably would not be able to satisfy all your children all the time. Decide what you can do for each child during each academic year (or month) and then stick to it. They may complain until they're thirty, but they'll eventually see the light. It may be the conflict they sense in you they are responding to. Conviction breeds acceptance.

I work at home, in an office we made out of an extra bedroom, and no matter how seriously I take my work, the world regards me as available. I yearn for a nice clean break so that I don't always have to apologize for my working time. How do other women isolate themselves so they are not put upon by the nonworking world in the middle of the day—a group which includes my family?

Many women/mothers find it difficult to work at home without interruption, guilt, or a sense of the separation between work and family time; yet men have offices in their homes (doctors, lawyers, professors, tradesmen, and a whole range of professional consultants) without the same problems, or without taking the problems so seriously.

Making the break into the work world may be as much psychological as logistical. Do you have a work phone, or do you have to use the home phone? Most men use a separate number for their work; why not women? Do you expect to be interrupted by a housekeeper, a child, a husband? Does your husband expect the same? Ask your husband to tell you how he would manage to make the same break and then do it his way. If he tells you that he would expect the household, including his wife, to *see to it* that only the fire department could break down his door, insist on the same treatment.

I'm forty-two and going back to work soon. My kids are in high school. Is there any special time of year that would be best—I'm looking for work as a secretary.

January. Christmas vacation and shopping is over; the kids are settled back into their school schedule. They will all be busy for the next five months and so will you.

When I pick my child up at his day-care center, he is exhausted, cranky, and hardly able to walk. He falls apart, wants me to carry him, fusses at me immediately. Is this common?

It is the most common thing in the world. Keep in mind a number of things as you struggle with this period: Even adults are tired at this time of day, especially those who have worked, gone to school, or dealt with other people away from home all day—all things your little boy has been doing at a much more rapid speed than any adult. His fussing at you, hitting you, complaining to you, nagging and demanding is his way of relating to the person he most loves and with whom he most feels at home.

But how to cope? By carrying him a bit, pampering him a bit, and then calling a halt to the scene when you can see that even he has had enough of it. (Easy to say, right? Don't be ashamed if some days you can't manage it.) Stay confident, firm, and consistent. He knows already that he's misbehaving and isn't fooled by a phony understanding kiss and tight-lipped grin. If you fall apart and get angry, he at last knows just how you feel—the same way he does.

Also, if the behavior persists or gets worse, ask yourself if you are sure the day-care center is giving him a low-key afternoon. Talk with his teachers and find out how they arrange the last two hours of the day. If they are aware of his fatigue, they may be able to help by offering him only very quiet, noncompetitive activities, like story time, listening to records, and the like.

Also arrange to have his father, if possible, come to pick him up for a while. Having run through his repertoire with you, he may have a whole new reaction to his father—a good way to diffuse everyone's anxiety.

I'm a nursing/working mother and I can get home in the middle of the day for a quick nurse and lunch. But lately my baby is trying to increase the amount of milk and wants to suck more often. Will I be inhibiting this reaction by still regulating my nine to five nursing time to that one noontime feeding?

Yes and no. Yes, you probably won't make much more milk than he takes during that nine to five period, but if you allow him to nurse as much as he wants the rest of the time, the flow will increase for the rest of the day, and night. Your breasts are the best twenty-four-hour clocks in the world and they learn quickly when to shut off the 2 A.M. feeding and when to turn on the 7 A.M. They will get the message from the increased feedings in the sixteen hours you are not at work.

If you have trouble meeting this new demand (the most common cause is fatigue), you could gently introduce some solid food. Many women also try expressing some milk manually during office hours. Millions of women work and nurse; don't be put off by stories of women who claim it can't be done.

My husband and I work eighteen hours a day, six days a week, and love it. Of course, we do want children soon, and want some advice about hiring a good mother substitute to be in the home, live in. What qualifications should we look for?

It's possible that you shouldn't have children on your schedules. You don't leave yourself enough time to be parents, at least not the kind that can bring up a healthy, happy, loved child. Ask yourself why you want a child and be sure you do want one before you have one.

I'm divorced, with three children to care for and a full-time job. Although I'm always very busy, the nights are lonely and the weekends are exhausting catch-up times which leave me feeling isolated from the rest of the adult world. I'm thinking of selling our house and moving into a condominium complex with young couples. But I'm afraid the move will alarm my children, who are seven, nine, and eleven—so soon after my divorce. What do you think?

How the move affects your children will probably depend on how good it will be for them in the new place—are there lots of other children around, good recreational facilities, good schools, opportunities for independent activities?

But a word of caution—many newly divorced mothers say they have a tendency to feel victimized in the first few years after their divorce. They see most of the world as married, happy, and barricaded behind a closed door called "couples." There is a tendency to assume that couples are better off so they ought to be able to befriend those who aren't. Their experience suggests that you ought not to expect too much from the couples in that condominium complex. They may be weighted down by their own involvements within those marriages that look so good from the outside. Furthermore they always have to be sensitive and responsive to each others' moods and needs, so they may not be too responsive to yours.

Many newly divorced women say their jobs offer them adult companionship; others plan for more contact, on their own initiative. Finding a select group of adults, either divorced like yourself or half and half, who choose to locate near each other or live communally may be another solution to consider.

fourteen

WHAT'S NEXT

Social change in the roles women play will of course continue to take place but, at the moment at any rate, Women's Liberation is operating less as active leadership in such change and more as an expressive demonstration that a good deal of change has already happened. How fast further steps that will affect more than a few women are going to be taken depends on how willing women are to tackle the unpleasant job of changing their image (including their self-image) and their behavior. Many of them will continue to put up with treatment that radical women deplore . . . because they are used to putting up with things. The old tradition teaches them to get their own back deviously instead of through straightforward confrontation on issues, and this is a lesson that is hard to unlearn. ELIZABETH JANEWAY, Man's World, Woman's Place, Morrow, 1971*

The problems of being a working mother, of living with a working mother, have been emphasized throughout much of this book. There are, however, many women, many families, who manage things well, who have few struggles with each other as a result of their busy lives, and who, furthermore, have found that two working parents can offer special rewards to every member of the family. I'm remembering all the women I met who had arranged their lives so efficiently that I wondered, at first, if they hadn't missed something by passing over all the indecision I knew so many other families and women were immersed in. On the contrary, these women, I discovered, were, as a result of careful planning, free to pursue a wide range of adult pleasures. They were more relaxed, more productive at their jobs, happier with their roles as mother and wife, and, not surprisingly, financially secure at a time when most couples are still struggling to save for a first mortgage.

One woman in a western Massachusetts suburb seemed, to me, to have an ideal arrangement. DeeDee and her husband had been put on the right track even before they met each other. Both of their mothers had worked. DeeDee's mother had been a social worker in New York City, and she had urged her daughter to find a career for herself from the time DeeDee was in grammar school. "Career counseling," DeeDee told me, "started, for me, in the cradle." Her father, a doctor, encouraged his daughter as well, and, she told me, provided an excellent model in the house for the husband of a working wife. "He did a lot of housework, and took care of us a lot of the time. I had a very happy childhood as a result."

DeeDee's husband, John, had grown up in a similar family situation. He had two sisters and a brother, a working mother, and a father who wanted all four of his children to grow up and have a profession. "I can remember supper hours when daddy would drill us on vocabulary tests before we could get dessert," John told me. "He felt we would never get anywhere without a strong vocabulary and a good American accent. As an immigrant Jew, that was probably understandable, but maybe it was unusual for him to encourage my sisters so much. They are both working mothers now, one a lawyer, one an English professor. It paid off."

There were no sex-role definitions in John's home either. Boys and girls helped both parents do the housework. John's description of the family's house cleaning could fit into a Marlo Thomas script. "Saturday morning and Tuesday night we all cleaned the house. Daddy would get home early that night, on Tuesday, afraid that mom would be tired. She was a bookkeeper and had a bad back. He lined us up and assigned us our chores and we had no supper until everything was done. We were so hungry that we'd work like demons. Then, we'd all go out to a delicatessen for some good kosher food. I never felt grudging about any of those cleaning days. We really had a very good time at it, and six of us could clean that apartment very quickly."

John and DeeDee met each other during their freshman year at college. They dated, fell in love, and decided to get married *after* they graduated. Come graduation they hit their first problem. She got a fellowship to Yale for graduate work; he got one to Harvard. "After much agony," DeeDee told me, "I decided I would try to commute. We announced our decision and my father said, 'That's a lousy way to start a marriage. You want a fellowship. . . . I'll give you a fellowship, to Harvard. You'll never finish your graduate work if you start out married and tired and not seeing enough of each other, I know.' So in a sense, my parents supported our marriage as much as they did my career. They liked the idea of John and me."

It took John and DeeDee six years to finish their educations. During that time they decided not to have children until she had her degree and had a job, which is exactly what happened. When I met them they had two children and both had jobs they enjoyed. "One interesting thing about our lives is that by my working," DeeDee said, "John has had an opportunity to take a research position he really wanted but which pays less. In that sense, my job has made a great difference in both our lives."

John and DeeDee share the management of the household in much the same way their parents did. The only difference they feel between their household and their parents' is that theirs is not as neat. "Things are always a bit hectic and we don't mind a bit of a mess. We probably react also to the perfect-house syndrome which I find aesthetically stifling. So we do with a lot of plants and tables strewn with paraphernalia. It's our style."

When they bought their first house, they selected it for its good schools, the availability of an excellent day-care center, its proximity to both their jobs and to public transportation. For the first few years, they used the day-care center for both children; one was three months old when he started. "Those were the best years for all of us. I never had any fears that things would not work out logistically, and the boys thrived. Our youngest had more intimate and trained care from the staff there, and from the other little children who loved to watch the babies then he would ever have received from me or a baby-sitter. He is very precocious and we feel the stimulation he received at such an early age helped tremendously to feed his constantly curious mind."

When the youngest was ready for kindergarten, they hired a live-in housekeeper who gets four weeks paid vacation a year, a cost of living raise once a year, and social security paid up. "We regard our housekeeper professionally," John told me. "Although we are warm and personal with her, we keep our family times private and allow her privacy too. This way she can have a life of her own and the work relationship is clear. With the children, she is wonderful, developing a rapport with them that is hardly professional. Now that they're older, and in school every day, she stays involved in their lives by planning afternoon things to do with them. They have both learned to be potters—a craft she taught them."

John and DeeDee are alive and real. I think of them often as I ponder the messages in this book. They are not alone in their success. I found many variations on their arrangement. For most couples, I found, the magic ingredient in a happy household with two working parents is an equal regard for each other's work. Men and women, I learned, who see their right to work as equal, and therefore respect the integrity of whatever work they do, find that equality in domestic and childrearing roles follows quite naturally. Equality so recognized, of course, is not a series of strict reckonings—"You take out the trash today; I'll make the beds." "I changed the last diaper; you get the next one." Equality for many couples is a state of mind that shapes the business of marriage, childrearing, and work, imbues them with rights as well as duties, respect along with competition.

Many husbands and wives I met found it difficult, however, to change their marital assumptions in midstream. Women without jobs or degrees, married to men earning high salaries and endowed with the proper certifications of technical or academic proficiency, are often reluctant to assert their equal right to pursue outside interests with the same psychological space their husbands enjoy. Nor do men, I found, easily recognize the need to take their wives' professional prospects as seriously as their own, especially if their wives' professional aims do not, on the surface, meet the highest standards of ambition. If one partner in a marriage earns a lot of money (in the popular mythology), then that partner and his (her?) needs deserve primary consideration. This assumption, I came to see, has led us to place a financial value on our roles as men and women, husbands and wives, mothers and fathers—one reason, women tell me, they have been dissatisfied with the limited appeal of housewifery.

The result is a distortion of human values, a distortion that women who have tasted life's possibilities want urgently to correct. Their aim, I believe, is less a reversal of the situation than the elimination of the old beliefs that sustain it.

If two parents are to work, they argue, let's put a higher value on childrearing than we have in the past. Let's stop arguing over *who* is going to spend time with the children; let's accept the indisputable fact of two parents, as well as the importance of childrearing, and raise them, together, with as much foresight and industry as we can manage.

The argument that the children of working mothers suffer is, in these women's experience, a myth. Children, they have found, can thrive with a mother and father off at work. The argument that they cannot, many women feel, stems from a fear of change and inexperience with anything but a standard, old-fashioned arrangement of family life.

On the other hand, if a woman wants to stay home with her children during their earliest years, most women say, she ought to feel self-confident, valued, and assured that when she decides to try something else, to enter the world of work, she will be taken seriously. But, they emphasize, the shift in parental and marital responsibility that follows ought not to come as a rude shock or a threatening possibility to her husband. He should know what it is to be an equal parent even while she is at home.

Likewise, women who choose to work immediately after childbirth want to be supported in their decision—by their husbands, relatives, neighbors, friends, and their doctors. Pediatricians and gynecologists, they say, should stop handing out advice calculated to put women on the defensive.

Women who do not work but want to, who are already in the midst of marriage and the childrearing years, face no easy answers or solutions. Many choose to live with whatever they honestly think they can absorb into their lives, without damaging themselves or their families. Of the range of possibilities, the women I talked with felt none is easy, or clean cut.

Women who recognize the need for change in their lives, yet fear the consequences for their marriage, sometimes move quietly and privately into a world of their own, so as not to rock any boats, not to confront any disorienting marital assumptions. Some find the work they want, and manage their domestic affairs well. The danger is that as they disguise, more and more, the women they are becoming, their husbands cling hopefully to the image of the women their wives used to be. I found that the consequences of this mutual deception—based on the false hope that a wish denied is a wish forgotten—were not always smooth. Some women, the more secure, move beyond their husbands, lose touch with them, and finally lose interest in them. Others, unable to transcend their frustrations, choose the course of resignation, timidity, and, for some, self-hatred.

Some women, I found, try the opposite path—direct confrontation—only to find themselves struggling alone. These women, in the past, have borne too heavy a price for their courage. They have raised their children alone, in a world that insists it can't be done, while pursuing their professions in a business world that never welcomed them. Psychic stress, they argue, comes not from a balanced and busy life, but from a social rigidity that tears at one's right to that life.

Women will choose, rightly or wrongly, with their husbands, or without them, most often in some gray area between. But their choice—the fact of these decisions, however they are made—will affect the generation of sons and daughters that follow us. They are the ones who can benefit most from this re-examination of roles and family life. They will inherit our legacy, the history of our time.